The American

STAPLERS, STAPLING MACHINES, & PAPER FASTENERS

volume 1

E.H. HOTCHKISS COMPANY OFFICE AND INDUSTRIAL STAPLING MACHINES

INCLUDING FASTENERS FROM JONES MANUFACTURING CO., COMPO MANUFACTURING & SALES, AND THE STAR PAPER FASTENER CO.

COMPLETE WITH ALL KNOWN VARIANTS

by Frank Parsons

Print Edition
★★★★
21/08

©2017-2021 Frank Parsons. All rights reserved. No part of this book may be reproduced in any form or by any electronic or mechanical means, including information storage and retrieval systems, without permission in writing from the author. Copyright registered with the U.S. Copyright Office, Washington D.C.

All photographs used are ©2017-2021 Frank Parsons unless otherwise credited.

Dedicated to my wife and true love. Without her support and understanding this project could never have happened.

Special thanks to "the Erudite Ogre" John Stevens for his editing work and general authorship help. If you see poor grammar or other issues it's probably because I didn't listen to him when I should have.

And thanks also to the Right Reverend Theodore (Ted) Munk. He spurred me on to create a bigger, better, and much more informative book. His experience and advice couldn't be more appreciated.

CONTENTS

INTRODUCTION 1

E.H. HOTCHKISS COMPANY 3

HOTCHKISS FASTENERS 5

JONES MANUFACTURING COMPANY 48

JONES MANUFACTURING COMPANY FASTENERS 49

COMPO MANUFACTURING & SALES COMPANY 51

COMPO MANUFACTURING & SALES COMPANY FASTENERS 52

STAR PAPER FASTENER COMPANY INC. 59

STAR PAPER FASTENER COMPANY INC. FASTENERS 60

STAPLER ANATOMY 75

STAPLE REMOVERS 77

STAPLE ANATOMY 78

STAPLE CLINCHING 80

STAPLES 82

ADVERTISEMENTS 93

INTRODUCTION

When I first started seriously collecting I recall looking on the internet for information on my various fasteners and not finding anything. Around 2001 I discovered two sites: the Early Office Museum and another site. The latter wasn't particularly helpful but the Early Office Museum, on the other hand, was an amazing website and an oasis in a desert of information. However, while the Early Office Museum provided a large breadth of information I found myself wanting something more in-depth.

Around 2009 I discovered the Stapler of the Week blog. This was like a breath of fresh air. The author didn't try to recount the history of an item but essentially wrote about his impressions of the fastener itself and what made it special to him. He also mixed it up and wrote about whatever stapler seemed to move him at the time. What made this site special was the obvious passion the author had.

In 2012 I decided to try my hand at a website dedicated to vintage and antique staplers. It would have passion and it would have as much information as I could find. It was awful. Within two months I deleted all the work I had done and told myself that I wasn't going to try that again.

A year went by and I couldn't get the idea of a website for those interested in staplers and other office equipment out of my head. So in February 2013 I started writing some articles but this time I concentrated on one specific item at a time and researched it as much as I could. I made sure to note my sources so others could see that what I had written was backed up with documentation. Within a few weeks I had written several articles I felt were passable and after some design work opened up the American Stationer blog.

What started out as a hobby has grown into an endeavor that has become more popular than I ever could have imagined. It seems that I wasn't the only one in the world who wanted to know a little bit more about these everyday objects that, while hardly noticed, have become indispensable office items.

And when it came to indispensable office items, E.H. Hotchkiss was arguably the "800 pound gorilla" of the stapler world when the company was active. For many collectors, the early Hotchkiss No 1, No 2, No 3 and No 4 fasteners are the crown jewels in a collection. The Zephyr is considered a must-have while the No 54 plier stapler with its geometric designs is a work of art. The most expensive stapler that I researched was a Hotchkiss H-31. You cannot consider yourself a serious collector without a Hotchkiss in your collection.

And that's where this book comes in. Use it. Use it to help you find staplers. Use it to identify staplers in your collection. Use it to help other collectors. It's taken me many years and much searching to compile this information. I can't think of anything more satisfying than to hear that this book was the most useful piece of information you had regarding fasteners.

I wish you the best of luck in your collecting!

E.H. HOTCHKISS COMPANY

The E.H. Hotchkiss Company was started in 1897 when, several years after first investing in the company, Eli H. Hotchkiss gained control of the Jones Manufacturing Company and changed the company's name.

Sometime between 1952 and 1954 Vail Manufacturing took a controlling interest in the E.H. Hotchkiss Company and by 1960 Hotchkiss-branded staplers were no longer being sold. ACCO acquired Vail Manufacturing in 1966.

There were a number of important people behind the success of Hotchkiss and their fasteners, although not all of them were directly involved with Hotchkiss. People such as Eli H. Hotchkiss himself, Edwin Greenfield, James Keyes, Fridolin Polzer, and Alexander H. Irvin had a significant role in bringing these fasteners to the market.

Eli H. Hotchkiss was the E.H. Hotchkiss for which the company was named. He bought into the Jones Manufacturing Company during a period of financial difficulty and within a few years had a controlling interest. Eli ran the company until his death in 1917 at which point his wife and father-in-law took control.

Edwin Greenfield and James Keyes were engineers/inventors who were responsible for much of the earliest designed staplers that Hotchkiss offered, including the No. 1. However, they never worked for Jones Manufacturing or for Hotchkiss directly. Fridolin Polzer was the engineer responsible for many of the staplers introduced through the 1920's and 1930's.

Moreso than any other single individual, Alexander H. Irvin was the secret to the early success of the Star Paper Fastener and to Hotchkiss. When stationers around the U.S. stopped ordering the Star Fastener A.H. Irvin, the original sales agent for Jones and then Hotchkiss, single-handedly increased sales, improved the company's reputation, and made the modern stapler a "staple" in every office around the world. Irvin was also the sales agent for Compo and ended up manufacturing his own brand of staplers. You'll see his name on the sides of a number of different fasteners.

Eli H. Hotchkiss  *Edwin Greenfield*  *Alexander Irvin*

HOTCHKISS FASTENERS

No 1
Version 1, without tail, plain plunger

Introduced in 1898 this was advertised through 1921 but would have been available longer. This weighed 1 pound 2 ounces and was made of nickel-plated cast iron. It measured 4 inches long by 2 inches wide by 4.5 inches high. Uses Hotchkiss No 1 staple strips. This is a very common stapler which is easy to find anywhere.

No 1
Version 1, without tail, stamped on plunger "Zion Office Supply". Picture is of plunger cap

All Hotchkiss No 1 staplers had plain plungers. The plunger stamps were an add-on by sellers. Made of very thin steel, brass, or nickel-plated brass, these would have been crimped on to the plunger handle afterwards.

No 1

Version 1, without tail, stamped on plunger "The National Office Supply Co". Picture is of plunger cap

Staplers with this plunger top are uncommon.

No 1

Version 1, without tail, stamped on plunger "H & W B Drew Co". Picture is of plunger cap

Founded in 1855 in Jacksonville, Florida, the H. & W. B. Drew Co. is still in business as Wells & Drew Company.

No 1

Version 1, with & without tail, stamped on plunger "The National Cash Register Co". Picture is of plunger cap

The most common of all plunger stamps by a long shot. The National Cash Register Company (NCR) was allowed not only to put their stamp on the plungers of No 1's but they were even sold in specially marked NCR boxes with NCR information on them.

No 1
Version 1, without tail, plain plunger, HY & Co

This is a Hotchkiss No 1 but manufactured by HY & Co. It is the same dimensions as the Hotchkiss built No 1 but is 3 ounces heavier. Note design differences; engraved line around Hotchkiss No 1, no decorative engraving on tail end of body, inscribed vertical lines on rear hinge, picket design on edge of base, and a logo of the letters "S" superimposed on a "Y" inside a horizontally aligned diamond shape surrounded by the words "HOTCHKISS PAPER FASTENER".

No 1
Version 1, with tail, plain plunger

Identical to its sibling in every way except for the addition of a staple-holding coil. The spiral coil adds another 2.75 inches to the overall length. Uses Hotchkiss No 1 staple strips.

No 1

Version 2, without tail, plain plunger. All version 2 fasteners had a black enameled base

Advertised in 1920 and 1921 but likely was around a couple of years before and after this time. It weighs 1 pound 2 ounces and measures 3.875 inches long by 1.938 inches wide by 4.438 inches high. Like all versions of the No 1 this uses Hotchkiss No 1 staple strips. No longer made of cast iron the body of this version is now a zinc compound.

No 1

Version 2, without tail, stamped on plunger "A.W. McCloy Co". Picture is of plunger cap

Founded by Albert Walter McCloy Sr. in 1879 in Pittsburgh, Pennsylvania. This company was one of the largest and most respected stationers in the area.

No 1
Version 2, with tail, plain plunger

catalog illustration

While the version 2 without the spiral coil is fairly common, this version with the coil is rare.

No 1
Version 3, without tail, plain plunger

This version, as far as I can tell, was never advertised. The body was made of a poor quality zinc and with a much squarer, and structurally weaker, design than version 2, these had a tendency to crack and break. They were likely pulled off the shelves almost as soon as they were released. This version is difficult to find in any condition. If you find one in good condition, and you're tempted to try it out, please don't. The resulting cracking and breaking of the metal will match the breaking of your heart as you realize that you've just destroyed a very rare stapler. It also uses Hotchkiss No 1 staple strips. But DON'T put staples in this. Or use it. Just don't. These weigh 1 pound 6 ounces empty and measure 3.75 inches long by 1.875 inches wide by 4.75 inches tall.

No 1

Version 3, without tail, stamped on plunger "The National Office Supply Co". Picture is of plunger cap

The National Office Supply Company had a long history with Hotchkiss. It isn't unusual to find version 3 No. 1 fasteners that are falling apart but with the plunger in near mint condition. They were so poorly made that many times the plunger would look like it had never been used.

No 1

Version 3, with tail, plain plunger

Identical to its sibling in every way except for the addition of a staple-holding coil. The spiral coil adds another 3 inches to the overall length.

No 1
Version 3, with tail, stamped on plunger "The National Cash Register Co". Picture is of plunger cap

NCR had a relationship with Hotchkiss and had NCR branded Hotchkiss No 1's through until the mid 1920's.

No 1
Version 4, without tail, plain plunger, pierced logo base

Models of the fourth version introduced between 1921 and 1924 had a base with the H logo pierced. It is also stamped "PATENT PENDING" on the bottom. This stapler weighs 1 pound 2 ounces and measures 3.875 inches long by 1.938 inches wide by 4.188 inches high. The body and base are made from a zinc composite with other parts made of steel. This stapler uses Hotchkiss No 1 staple strips.

No 1
Version 4, without tail, plain plunger, pierced logo base

Available starting in 1925 and available until approximately 1930. Logo on base is pierced. Bottom of base inscribed "PAT. JAN 20, 1925" and "OTHERS PENDING". This is a common stapler but in order to properly date it you will need to check what is inscribed on the underside of the base.

No 1
Version 4, without tail, plain plunger, solid logo base

Available starting around 1930, this model was advertised as late as 1946 but was likely available for years after that. Bottom of base inscribed "PAT. JAN 20, 1925" and "OTHERS PENDING". Both this version with the solid logo base and with the pierced logo base are common and easy-to-find staplers.

No 1
Version 4, without tail, plain plunger, black hammerloid paint finish

This model with the black finish would have been available from approximately the late 1930's until the 1940's. While the version 4 is an easy enough stapler to find, one with this finish is extremely rare.

No 1
Version 4, without tail, plain plunger, black hammerloid body with chrome base

This version seems to be just a bit easier to find than the all black one, but it is still a rare and difficult to find model.

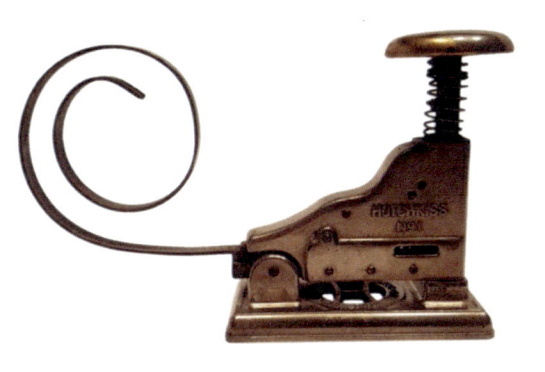

No 1
Version 4, with tail, plain plunger, pierced logo base

Identical to its siblings in every way except for the addition of a staple-holding spiral coil. The spiral coil adds another 3 inches to the overall length.

No 1
Japanese version

This is listed in a 1922 Japanese supply catalog. I'm unsure how common these are in Japan, but they are very rare in the United States. This was manufactured by the Japanese company of I.T.K & Co of Osaka. Although sold in Japan all wording on both the fastener and the box are in English.

No 1A
Original version, nickel-plated

First advertised in 1927, the No 1A was the first of the new generation of Hotchkiss fasteners. This model boasted a huge (compared to the original No 1) staple capacity of 210 staples, an all new patented feed mechanism, and a plunger that took much less force to staple with as compared to its older strip stapler siblings. They even built a ruler into the base. It does not however have the adjustable anvil found in later versions. It's something of a mystery why Hotchkiss called this model the "1A" instead of starting from where they left off and calling this the model 6. Such are the mysteries of life. This version was sold through 1931 and is rare.

No 1A
Chrome

First seen in 1932, the new 1A added some mechanical and cosmetic improvements including an adjustable anvil that allowed you to make permanent and temporary fastenings. This is a fairly common stapler and one that is easy to find in good condition. It uses modern standard staples so is a good choice for those looking to add a vintage touch to their desk.

No 1A
Chrome with black hammerloid paint finish

The No 1A weighs a hefty 2 pounds 2 ounces empty and measures 7.25 inches long by 2 inches wide by 4.25 inches tall. The 1A series was advertised starting in 1927 and was available until Hotchkiss was taken over by Vail in the 1950's. The model 1A is a common stapler and is extremely well-made. Those looking for a usable vintage desk stapler will find this to be an excellent choice.

catalog illustration

No 1A
Black hammerloid enamel body and base with chrome plunger

The black hammerloid paint would have been introduced in the mid-to-late 1930's and would have been the only choice through the war. This version of the model 1A is a bit more difficult to find then the version with the chrome base and is uncommon.

Hotchkiss No 1A / Star No '31
Black hammerloid enamel body and base with copper plated plunger, block, screws

This is likely a one-off hybrid of a Hotchkiss 1A body on a Star '31 base. However, it shows that these models existed in copper plate. Furthermore, the wear patterns show that this pairing were together from the very beginning, possibly even from the factory. This is the only copper plated fastener of any kind seen for Hotchkiss, Star or Compo making this an exceptionally rare piece.

No 2
Marked Hotchkiss No 2 on side

Made of 4 pounds of nickel-plated iron and a wooden handle, this is one serious fastener. The No 2 measures 10.25 inches long by 2.75 inches wide by 8 inches tall. This uses the No 2 Hotchkiss staple strip and was rated to staple from 2 to 50 pieces of paper. I would consider this an uncommon fastener but it shows up regularly for sale. The base is highly decorative with the fastener and lever mechanism only slightly less ornamental. Advertisements have been found from 1903 to 1923 but it is likely to have been sold at least until 1930. By 1936 the next generation of the No 2 (the No 2 version 2) was being exclusively advertised.

No 2
Marked Hotchkiss No 3 on side

If you look closely at the No 2 you'll notice that this is really just a No 3 with the base and plunger removed and replaced by a much larger base and a lever. When the No 2 was first introduced Hotchkiss simply took No 3 staplers, changed parts, and gave it a new model number. In an article in the October 1903 issue of the Book-Keeper you can clearly see a Hotchkiss No 2 but with the stapler marked Hotchkiss No 3. This version is rare and more difficult to find then it's later versions which were clearly marked on the side as Hotchkiss No 2.

No 2
version 2, nickel plated

The second generation of the No 2 is even heavier than the first weighing in at 5 pounds empty. It measures 11 inches long by 2.5 inches wide by 10 inches high. It is made of cast iron and steel and uses both the No 2 and No 4 strip staples. The No 2 was available from office suppliers and was advertised from about 1925 to 1936 but was likely available for a short time after this. For such a heavy fastener the mechanics on this are surprisingly smooth and give you the feeling that you can staple anything. This is a very rare version of the No 2.

No 2A

The model 2A is essentially a lower-capacity, smaller desktop version of the model 1A. It weighs 1 pound 8 ounces and measures 5.25 inches long by 2 inches wide by 4.25 inches tall. It has a capacity of 100 staples and uses standard-size staples. Available throughout the 1930's this is a common and reasonably easy-to-find stapler. Like the model 1A this is an excellent stapler if you are looking for a usable, vintage fastener for your desk.

No 2C
Chrome with grey hammerloid enamel

This model was essentially a heavy-duty version of the model 1A and was available in the 1950's.

No 3

Made of nickel-plated cast iron and like it's siblings was tough as nails. It used No 3 strip staples and was rated to fasten from 2 to 30 sheets of paper. Advertisements and references have been found from 1903 to 1923 but it is likely to have been sold until about 1930. This is a rare fastener but with some patience you'll see that it shows up regularly for sale on the internet.

No 3
version 2

The only difference between versions 1 and 2 is the base. Version 2 uses the same type of modernized design base as the No 4 version 3. This was likely available in the late 1920's and is a rare machine.

No 3A-54
Nickel-plated

Identical in nearly every respect to the model 3C-54. Uses Hotchkiss H.54 or H.52 staples.

No 3C-54
Nickel-plated

catalog illustration

The body, base and much of the fastener were made of nickel-plated zinc for this model with some of the parts made of steel. It weighs one pound and measures 4.4375 inches long by 1.75 inches wide by 3.375 inches tall. It uses the extra-small Hotchkiss No 52 or 54 staples. This is essentially the desktop version of the No 52 plier-type stapler. In appearance it seems like a smaller version of the model 2A, which was itself a smaller version of the model 1A. This doesn't seem quite so odd once you realize that all of these staplers were covered under the same patents. Available for a relatively short period in the 1930's this should be considered a rare stapler.

No 4
Version 1

Weighing 1 pound and 8 ounces and measuring 5.75 inches long by 1.9375 inches wide by 4.6875 inches tall the No 4 was made from nickel-plated cast iron. It was rated to staple from 2 to 40 sheets of paper and could hold a strip of 50 No 2/No 4 strip staples. This is a rare stapler to find in any condition.

box illustration

No 4
Version 2

This version of the No 4 has not been spotted in the wild. I only know of its existence because I have the box it would have come in. I wish I had the stapler too. This illustration is from the box cover.

No 4
Version 3

Weighing-in at 2 pounds of nickel-plated steel this is one hefty fastener. It measures 6.25 inches long by 2 inches wide by 5.5 inches tall. This is a contemporary of the version 3 No 2 heavy duty fastener and is most likely from the 1930's. This is an extremely rare version of the No 4, so rare that the one pictured is literally the only one I've ever seen.

No 5 Automatic Tag Machine
Nickel-plated cast iron

Advertisements from 1906 to 1922 have been found, but it is likely that it was around from 1903 until about 1930 much like the first version of the No 2. The No 5 weighs 1 pound 10 ounces and measures 5.25 inches long by 1.25 inches wide by 4 inches tall. This is a rare machine, not because there weren't many made but because these machines took a beating and not many survived. Like all of the early Hotchkiss fasteners this is nickel-plated cast iron. This machine also used strip staples.

No 5A
Version 1, nickel-plated

This particular variant is the oldest known for this model. Size, weight, staple capacity, etc. are the same as per later versions. However, there are three main differences; 1) the front lever or "dog" is covered by a screwed in plate (see photo); 2) the spring coil is covered by a removable plate that covers all the way to the staple guide and; 3) the block is larger than normal. Later variants would simply remove the front lever cover and leave it exposed, the spring coil cover would be cast as part of the body, and the block would be smaller and flush with the body. While the model 5A is a common stapler, this variant is rare.

No 5A
Version 1, chrome with black hammerloid enamel

Marked No 5 on the forward part of the base but this is really the 5A. This marking discrepancy is something that Hotchkiss is known for and it's unknown why they did it. However, it was advertised and sold as the model 5A and the box would have labeled it as a model 5A also. The version 1 of the model 5A weighs 1 pound and 7 ounces. It measures 7.4375 inches long x 2 inches wide x 4 inches high. The magazine held a strip of 210 standard size staples. This version was introduced about 1936 and available through the mid-1940's. It's a common fastener and one you'll run across regularly.

No 5A
Version 1, black hammerloid enamel body and base with chrome plunger only

While this stapler was as tough as they come, the black hammerloid enamel on the base had a tendency to chip rather than scratch. That means it's not unusual to see one of these hammerloid bases with lots of chipped paint. While the first version of the model 5A is a common stapler this color combination is more uncommon. It is especially difficult to find one with a base that has no chips.

No 5A
Version 1, grey hammerloid body and base

Towards the end of the 1940's Hotchkiss started moving away from the black hammerloid enamel and started using grey hammerloid. Like black hammerloid, grey also has a tendency to chip rather than scratch. This color combination is rare and difficult to find without any chipping.

No 5A
Version 2, chrome with grey hammerloid enamel

Version 2 of the model 5A was larger but weighed less. It was 1 pound 1 ounce and measures 8.125 inches long by 2.1875 inches wide by 4 inches tall. It still used standard size staples. According to sales literature it was designed for everywhere a stapling machine really "Takes a Beating." Available beginning in the 1950's, this version was introduced shortly prior to Hotchkiss being taken over by Vail Industries. So although it was popular for the years it was sold it is still an uncommon stapler.

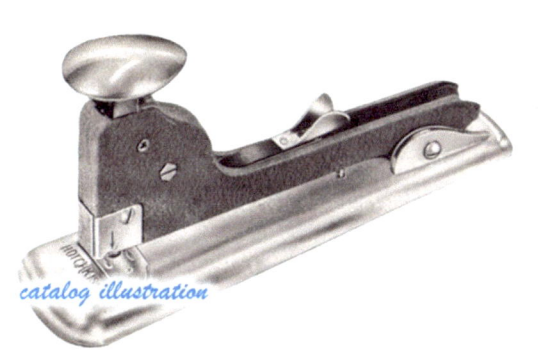

No 5A
Version 2, chrome with black hammerloid enamel

Besides size and weight, there are a few other design changes between the version 1 and version 2. Note that it now uses a flush anvil that you must lift and twist to change between permanent and temporary stapling. The plunger is approximately 25% larger. The base is now about a half inch longer and tapered. This fastener, the version 2 model 5A in black hammerloid, was likely introduced in the late 1940's. This is also an uncommon stapler.

No 5L
Chrome with black hammerloid enamel

With a "die-cast" base, frame and plunger, and a body made of pressed-steel, this model weighs 1 pound 10 ounces and measures 7.5 inches long by 2 inches wide by 4 inches tall. It is front-loading and holds up to 210 standard-size staples. Introduced in 1946 it was no longer in production by January 1956. It is a very well-made stapler and the design is simple and timeless but it seems to be "more of the same" from Hotchkiss. The forward part of the base is engraved "No 5" but the original box, all office suppliers, and all advertisements call this the model 5L. This is an uncommon stapler that will also be usable and good-looking on your vintage desk.

No 6A
Chrome. Marked on forward part of base as "NO 6" but model number is actually 6A

First known to be available in 1937. This fastener weighs 1 pound empty and measures 5.5 inches long by 2 inches wide by 4.125 tall. It can hold 105 standard staples and can handle multiple gauge wire. While the all chrome stapler isn't as easy to find as the black and chrome version, it is still a common fastener.

No 6A
Black hammerloid enamel with chrome base and plunger.

The model 6A was another in the Hotchkiss line's tough-as-nails staplers. With the sliding anvil it could form permanent or temporary staples. It could also be used as a tacker in which form it excelled. This color combination is the easiest to find and is a common stapler.

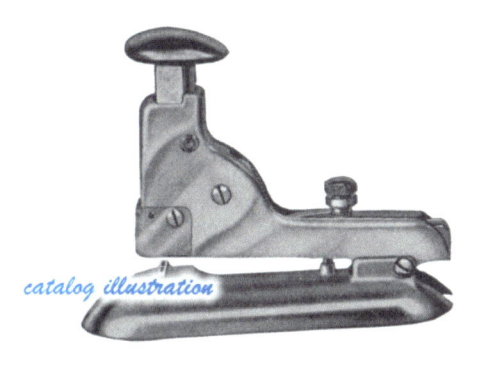

No 6A
Black hammerloid enamel body and base with chrome plunger only.

catalog illustration

While you will see this color combination regularly, it is not seen as often as the first two above. This is an uncommon fastener to find.

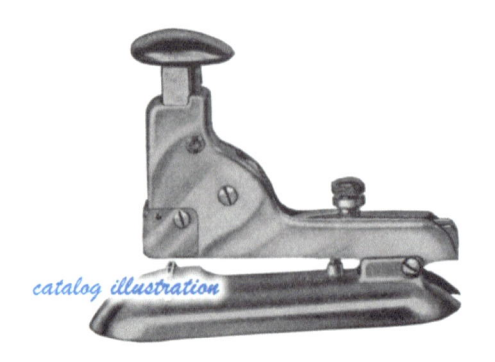

No 6A
Grey hammerloid enamel body and chrome

This color combination was only available in the mid-1950's. No other combinations were being sold at that time. This version of the 6A is rare.

No 10 Automatic Tacker

The No 10 was sold in the late 1930's through the early 1950's but it may have been available longer. This tacker measures 5.75 inches tall by 6.25 inches long by .95 inches wide and weighs 1 pound 12 ounces. It uses No 1 strip staples and holds 50 in its magazine. This is a rare fastener in any condition.

No 15 Comet Tacker
Chrome with grey hammerloid enamel

The Comet was designed for light construction and home maintenance tasks such as installing window screens, insulation, and upholstery. It uses special industrial-grade heavy-duty staples. It measures 7.5 inches long by 5.25 inches tall and weighs 1 pound 13 ounces. It's unknown what time period this tacker was available although it is known to have been sold in the mid-1950's. This is a common fastener but one that is difficult to find in good condition because of the manner in which it was used.

No 18 Star Tacker

The No 18 is finished in green hammerloid and chrome. It is made of "die cast" frame and body with hardened steel parts. "Die cast" is marketing speak for zinc alloy. It is the exact same size and weight as its sibling, the No 15 Comet. The only difference is that it uses a slightly different size industrial staple. This is an uncommon fastener and difficult to find in good condition due to the way it was designed to be used.

No 20 Director
Chrome

This is a rare fastener that was released around 1950 and was around until about 1955. It is the same weight as the 101A Zephyr at 1 pound 10 ounces, and is just about the same size at 8.375 inches long by 2.5 inches wide by 3.75 inches tall. It's chrome, made from 100% steel, rear loading, uses standard staples, has a neat rotating anvil with two settings and tacks. However, it's difficult to get over the fact that it's an also-ran in the looks department. It tries to be what the Zephyr was but doesn't quite get it. If the Zephyr and the Bantam hooked-up, this would be their love child.

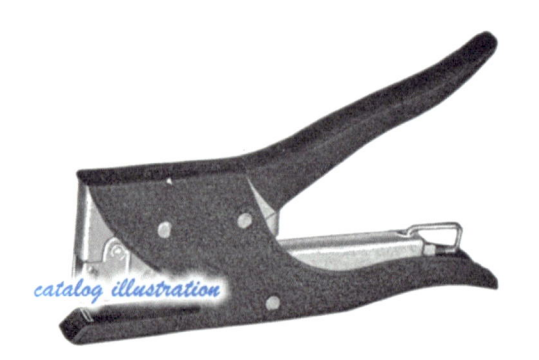

No 51
Identical in appearance to the No 53 except uses thicker staples

catalog illustration

Hotchkiss considered both the No 51 and No 53 to be industrial staplers. And it's no wonder. The No 51 plier stapler is a serious machine with a heft and feeling of durability that lets you know it plans to work harder than you. It weighs 1 pound 2 ounces and measures 7.5 inches long by 0.625 inches wide by 4 inches tall. The No 51 uses H.51 staples which have a crown of .4375 inch and a wire size of .025 (24 gauge) and has a capacity of 125 staples. This is an uncommon stapler to find and they are often beat up. The No 51 would have been more at home in a heavy commercial/light industrial setting and as such were heavily used on a regular basis.

No 52
Chrome

Available in 1936, the all-chrome version of the No 52 plier stapler was available until 1940 or 1941. This fastener weighs 8 ounces and measures 5.75 inches long by .5 inches wide by 2.9375 tall. The No 52 was a light-duty stapler that used tiny staples. As such its usefulness was mostly in homes and schools. However, where businesses needed a tiny flat staple this would have fit the bill so these turn up from time-to-time in old movie theaters and florists. This is an uncommon stapler to find in this finish.

No 52
Chrome with green hammerloid enamel

 It's difficult to fit this version into the No 52 timeline. However, some construction clues point to it being a contemporary of the all-chrome fastener. This is a rare fastener to find in this finish.

No 52
Chrome with black hammerloid enamel

The black hammerloid No 52 was available from 1942 at least through 1946, but probably longer. It uses H.52 or H.54 staples which have a 0.25 inch crown. The No 52 has a 70 staple capacity. This is a common fastener to find in this finish.

No 52
Chrome with grey hammerloid enamel

The grey hammerloid No 52 was available starting in the early 1950's and around until the late 1950's/early 1960's when Hotchkiss was no longer manufacturing staplers. This is a common fastener to find in this finish.

No 53
Chrome with black hammerloid enamel

Weighing 1 pound 2 ounces and measuring 7.5 inches long by 0.625 inches wide by 4 inches tall, the No 53 is a heavy-duty plier stapler that means business. This fastener uses No 53 plier staples or H.51 staples which have a crown of .4375 inch and a wire size of .025 (24 gauge) and has a capacity of 125 staples. This is an uncommon stapler to find in good condition. The No 53 was marketed to heavy commercial/light industrial customers and their condition often reflects the hard life they've led .

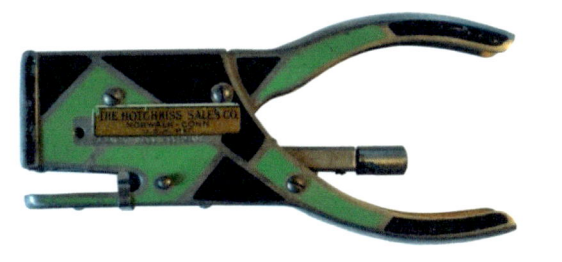

No 54
Nickel with green and black enamel in geometric pattern

German engineered and German manufactured, these highly decorative plier-type staplers were well-built, well-designed, and a pleasure to use. These are essentially rebranded Elastic Juwels which also sported similar geometric enamels in similar colors. The paint used on these isn't very durable and is easily scratched.

No 54
Nickel with white and black enamel in geometric pattern

The Juwel stapler is still made and the 21/4 staples they use will fit the No 54. You can also use Hotchkiss No 54 staples which were advertised as having a 1/4 inch crown.

No 54
Nickel with red and black enamel in geometric pattern

The No 54 measures 5.75 inches long by .5 inches wide by 2.75 inches high and weighs 6 ounces empty. All versions of the No 54 should be considered rare.

No 54
Nickel with orange and yellow enamel in geometric pattern

The No 54 is known to have been available from 1933 to 1938. It's possible that the No 54 was released as early as 1931 and sold up to about 1940, but it is extremely unlikely this model in any version was sold past 1940 unless the seller was simply dumping old stock. No stationer in the U.S. would want to be seen selling German-made merchandise by 1940.

No 54
Nickel-plated

Like all of its siblings, the nickel-plated No 54 was a light-duty stapler. However, despite the fact that this version was much shinier than the others it didn't share the same level of sales success. The nickel-plated No 54 plier stapler is a rare stapler.

No 57 True Blue Clipper
Chrome with blue enamel

The No 57 was known to be sold from 1937 through 1956. However, it is likely it was sold a couple of years earlier and later. It weighs 8 ounces empty and measures 5.75 inches long by 0.5 inches wide by 2.875 inches tall. The magazine held a strip of 70 H.57 or "Coronet" staples. These staples were extremely small and had a 0.25 inch crown. This is an uncommon stapler to find, but rare to find with the paint fully intact. Like its sibling, the No 54, the enamel quality was atrocious and wore quickly with even light use.

No 57
black flat enamel with black hammerloid enamel

Proudly made in Norwalk, Connecticut, and not Germany, the No 57 is amazingly similar to the No 54 which should be a problem because the No 54 was German made and therefore a licensed product. It becomes a bit clearer when you realize that the patent holder for the No 57 and the German designer and manufacturer of the No 54 were one and the same. This common thread was one Max Vogel. Max Vogel owned M. Vogel A.G., a German firm. In 1933 Vogel started a stapler firm in the U.S. - Neva-Clog in Bridgeport, Connecticut, just 15 miles from Hotchkiss. Mr.

Vogel, being Jewish, left Germany and soon after his company was renamed/taken-over by Elastic A.G. Mr. Vogel had the foresight to file his U.S. patents under his name, and not his company's, and was therefore in a position to assign his patent to Hotchkiss. The No 57 was covered under a second patent but this was the same one that seems to cover all of the Hotchkiss plier-type staplers.

No 96 Trojan Tacker

This early version of the Trojan Tacker measures 7.375 inches long by .938 inches wide by 6 inches high. It is made of chrome-plated steel and weighs one pound 12 ounces empty. Uses size 96 staples, either B or C depending on front plate. The front plate (which is removable) is located at the front end of the staple guide and will be inscribed with either the number 25 or 50. If it is inscribed with a 25 you must use 96B staples. If it is inscribed with 50 you must use 96C. This is a rare fastener.

No 101A Zephyr
Chrome with black hammerloid enamel

The Zephyr is an uncommon stapler that is extremely desirable. It's larger than the average stapler measuring 8 inches long by 2.125 inches wide by 3.25 inches high. It weighs-in at a hefty 1 pound 10 ounces empty. You can load 210 standard-size staples at a time into the front loading carrier allowing you to staple every day from January 1 until July 29. The Zephyr was available from office suppliers from 1940 until at least 1946.

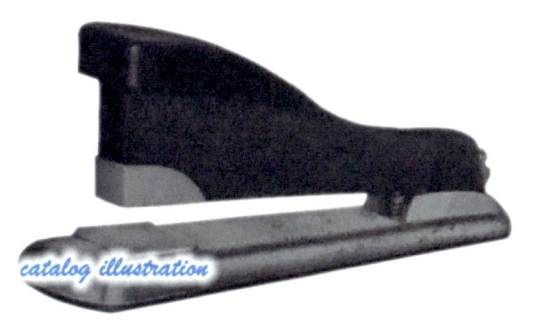

No 120A
Chrome with black hammerloid enamel

This fastener is 8.5 inches long by 2.125 inches wide by 3.25 inches tall. The body disconnects from the base for tacking. The magazine holds 210 standard size staples. The 120A has what Hotchkiss called a quadri-clinch anvil allowing for four different types of fastening. This is a common fastener.

No 122A Bantam
Chrome with black hammerloid

The Bantam is a small, light-duty desk stapler that measures 5 inches long by 1.75 inches wide by 2 inches high and weighs 8 ounces empty. It uses standard staples. You'll see this "swooping wedge" design on a number of Hotchkiss staplers from around this time including the Red Head, the Director, and the Zephyr. Some of these were advertised as having a rubber non-slip base but I've never seen one with this base intact. The lack of rubber feet could imply that some kind of rubber base was used. Advertised from 1945-1956 but was likely available for a few years both before and after this time period.

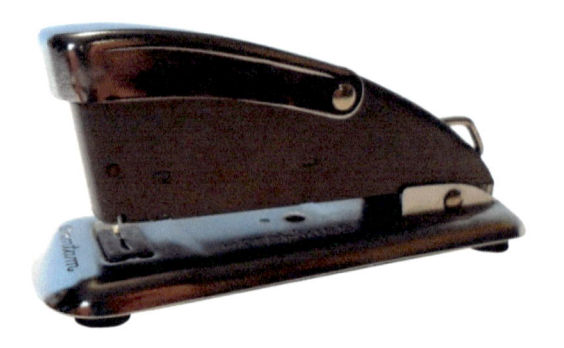

No 122A Bantam
Chrome with grey enamel

Identical in size and shape to the previous model, this can be identified as a later version. Note the word "Bantam" in script on the forward part of the base. Also note that there are now rubber feet.

No 122B
Chrome with black hammerloid enamel and plastic base

The only real difference between models 122A and 122B is the plastic base on the model 122B. It has the same dimensions at 5 inches long by 1.75 inches wide by 2.25 inches high and weighs 8 ounces empty. It holds 105 standard staples. One item to note though is that neither the stapler nor the original box refer to this fastener as the "Bantam". It is simply model 122B. While the model 122A was commonly available from office suppliers and heavily advertised, the model 122B was not generally available via office suppliers nor was it advertised. It was however sold during the same period as the model 122A. This is an uncommon stapler but especially so in good condition.

No 122P Bantam Plier
Nickel with black hammerloid enamel

The No 122P weighs 8 ounces and measures 4.25 inches long by 1 inch wide by 2.5 inches tall. Holds 105 standard size staples. This is a common stapler.

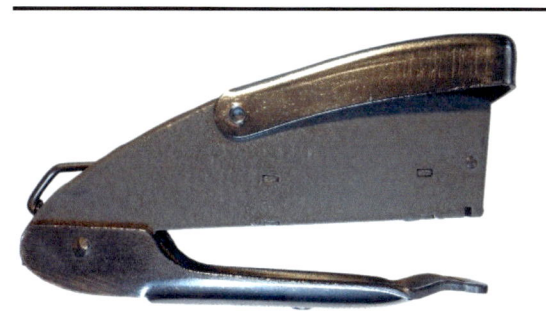

No 122P Bamtam Plier
Chrome with grey hammerloid enamel

The Bantam Plier was around for the same time period as the No 122A Bantam. It was advertised from 1945 - 1956 but was likely around for several years both before and after that timeframe.

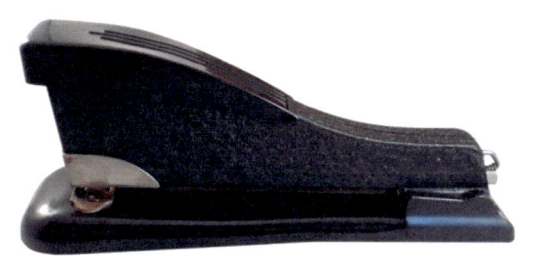

No 220
Black hammerloid enamel with black plastic base and plunger

This fastener is 8 inches long by 2.12 inches wide by 3 inches tall. The body disconnects from the base for tacking. The magazine holds 210 standard size staples. The body, anvil, and internal parts are steel while the base and plunger are black plastic. This stapler is known to have been available between 1937 and 1941 but it was likely available for a number of years both before and after. This is an uncommon stapler to find in general, but rare in good condition.

No D-96 Trojan Tacker

The model D-96 Trojan Tacker weighs 1 pound 13 ounces and measures 7.5 inches long by 5.25 inches high by 1.5 inches wide. It is finished in grey hammerloid and chrome. Uses Hotchkiss 96B or 96C staples. This tacker is a bit more difficult to find and should be considered uncommon.

No H-30 Red Head
Chrome with red and black hammerloid enamel

The H-30 measures 5.5 inches long by 1.5 inches wide by 2 inches high and weighs 8 ounces empty. It uses 6/4 staples that are smaller than the ones Hotchkiss used for the model 52 and 54 plier staplers. The 6/4 staples are about 2/3 the size of number 10 staples as a comparison. The H-30 was made of 100% steel with a chrome-plated operating lever and staple housing. The body was finished in a red crackle paint while the top of the base was in black crackle. Made for a very short time between 1937 and 1938, this model is very rare. This little beauty hits the "collecta trifecta" of cheap materials, odd proprietary sized staples that are (and were even then) hard to find, and a mechanism that jammed more than Bob Marley. It's no secret why this stapler is so rare.

No H-31 Aristocrat

catalog illustration

Available approximately 1937 and 1938, the Aristocrat used the same type of stapling mechanism as the H-30. It was larger than the H-30 and had a marbleized plastic cover over the stapling mechanism. This is an extremely rare machine.

No HA-1 / HA 12" Long Reach
Nickel plated stapler with grey base

When this long reach stapler was introduced it was called the model HA-1. It's difficult to say exactly when this model was available, but it was no earlier than 1927 (when the model 1A was introduced) and no later than 1937 by which time it was widely and easily available. By 1956 this fastener was simply called the model HA. This model is a rare fastener.

No HA-1 / HA 12" Long Reach
Black hammerloid stapler with grey base

The base is cast aluminum and bored for attaching to a bench or table. It weighs 4 pounds 9 ounces and measures 16.5 inches long by 2.6875 inches wide by 5.25 inches tall. Uses standard staples. This is a rare fastener.

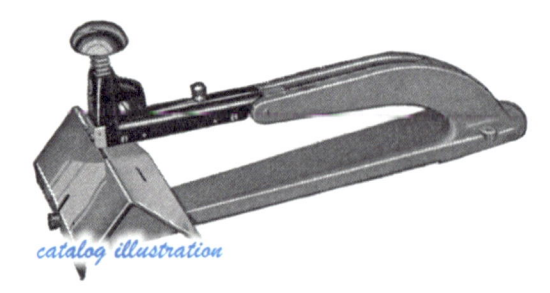

No HA Saddle Stitcher

Designed to staple books, pamphlets, etc. Loads 210 standard staples. Base is drilled for fastening to bench or table. Weighs 7.5 pounds and measures 17 inches long by 7 inches tall. Known to be available between 1937 and 1948, but likely available for years before and after this timeframe. This is a rare fastener.

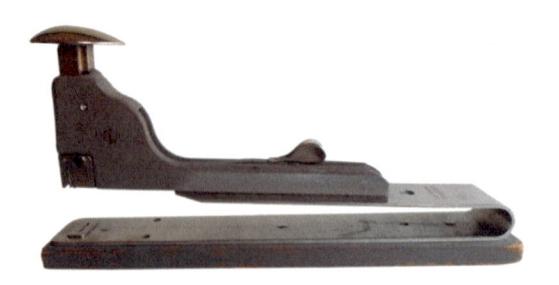

No HG-5 8" Long Range
grey hammerloid with chrome plunger and grey painted wood base

The HG-5 8 Inch Long Range weighs 1.5 pounds and measures 9.5 inches long by 1.5625 inches wide by 4.5625 inches high. It uses standard sized staples. The wood base is an integral part of the stapler and is riveted on to the bottom. This is a rare stapler.

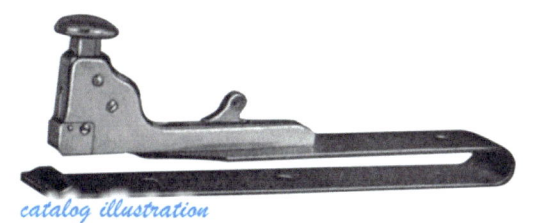

No HG-5 12" Long Range

catalog illustration

This is a No 5A Hotchkiss stapler mounted on a spring steel base. The base is pre-drilled for mounting on a bench or table. Loads 210 standard staples. This is an uncommon machine.

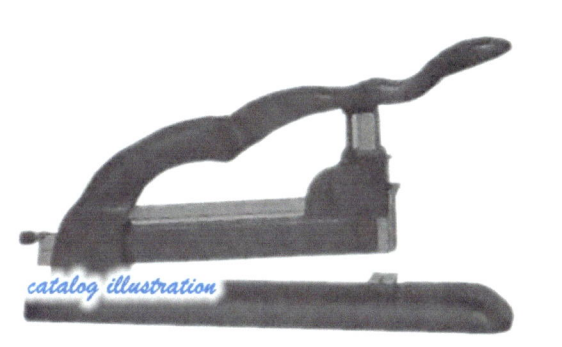

No L-40

catalog illustration

Made of an aluminum alloy construction and measuring 20 inches long by 3.5 inches wide by 10.5 inches tall. Uses heavy duty staples with 0.5 inch crown and 0.5 inch leg. First available in 1934. This is a rare fastener.

No S-18 Tacker
Green hammerloid enamel and nickel plate

Zinc alloy body with steel parts. Weighs 1 pound 13 ounces and measures 7.5 inches long by 5.25 inches tall. Holds a strip of 140 No 18 staples. This is an uncommon fastener and difficult to find in good condition.

Giant Star Fastener
Nickel-plated cast iron

Approximately twice the size of the smaller Star Fastener. This was made of nickel-plated iron. It would have been available in the same period as the Star Fastener. This is a rare fastener.

Stapl-On Hammer Stapler

Weighs 2 pounds and is made from steel with an aluminum handle. It measures 11.5 inches long by 1 inch wide by 3.5 inches tall. These were available starting in 1947 until at least 1956. This type of fastener is often used by roofers. There were two versions differentiated only by the leg length of the staples used. One used #25 and the other #25.5.

Star Fastener
Nickel-plated cast iron

The Star Fastener weighs 1 pound 6 ounces and measures 5.4375 inches long by 2.0625 inches wide by 4.6875 inches tall and is made of nickel-plated iron. This was the immediate successor to the Jones Mfg Co Star Fastener and the direct antecedent to the Hotchkiss No 1. If you place the three fasteners side-by-side the evolution is obvious. The Star has the distinction of being the first fastener sold under the Hotchkiss name. It also uses the No 1 strip staples. This was available 1898 to 1901 and is a rare fastener. However, A.W. McCloy Co of Pittsburgh, Pennsylvania, sold these as the "original No 1" as late as 1917.

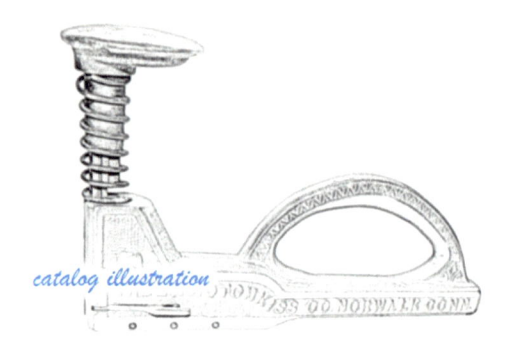

Tacker
Nickel-plated cast iron

A very early tacker/tag machine from Hotchkiss. This is a very rare machine.

Unit

The Unit was available from 1922 to 1925. This is a rare fastener but shows up for sale from time-to-time. It weighs 1 pound 10 ounces and measures 5 inches long by 2.375 inches wide by 4.5 inches high. The plunger is made of steel while the body and base are a zinc composite. All parts are nickel-plated. What made this fastener different is that it used both No 1 and No 2 staples and was rated to fasten up to 50 sheets. The Unit was also the first Hotchkiss strip-stapler that used screws in construction meaning it could easily be repaired. All previous models used steel dowels in construction which made them very difficult to repair.

JONES MANUFACTURING COMPANY

The earliest known advertisement for the Star Paper Fastener manufactured by the Jones Manufacturing Company is from 1895, although the company was around before then. The name of the company was changed to the E.H. Hotchkiss Company in 1897.

The Star Fastener was the only stapler made by the Jones Manufacturing Company. In 1897, the newly renamed E.H. Hotchkiss Company would continue manufacturing and selling the Star Fastener only now marked with the Hotchkiss name. During this short time Hotchkiss also released the Giant Star which was essentially the same machine only approximately 50% larger. In 1901 the Hotchkiss No. 1 was released and was the replacement model for the Star Fastener.

While Hotchkiss was no longer selling the Star Fastener after 1901 they did retain rights to the name and about 20 years later would start selling rebranded Hotchkiss staplers along with licensed German built plier-type staplers under the Star Paper Fastener Company name.

JONES MANUFACTURING COMPANY FASTENERS

Star Fastener

This may look like a dinosaur but it's more akin to the first homo sapiens. This is the precursor to all modern staplers and can be considered the first truly modern stapler. There were staplers before this one but they generally loaded only one staple at a time with the legs needing to be hand bent after insertion into the papers. The staples were prone to misalignment, bending before insertion into paper, and tearing the papers. If they held more than one staple at a time it was because they had to be fastened to a special rod or used some other difficult method. These fasteners ultimately were little more than glorified hammers.

The Jones Manufacturing Company Star Paper Fastener could hold dozens of staples without needing special rods, rubber bands, and other such. When you used a staple, a new staple was forwarded in the magazine and it was ready to go again. The anvil would bend the staples automatically so that they were bent to hold your papers. The mechanism was designed so that it seldom jammed. And it was totally self-contained. Everything you needed in order to staple was built into the fastener. All you added was staples as necessary. And it was the right size to be placed on your desk. You didn't need a special stand or training to use it. It was intuitive, easy-to-use, and it just plain worked.

Nowadays, you pick up your stapler, insert some paper, press down on the top and you now have a set of fastened papers. However, when the Star Fastener was introduced no other fastener did what it did in the way it did it. It wasn't from lack of trying, but the Star was the first success.

The Star weighs 1 pound and measures 5.5 inches long by 2.125 inches wide by 4.375 inches tall. It is made of nickel-plated iron and steel and uses the same strip staples as the Hotchkiss No 1.

The Star Fastener was available by 1895. When E.H. Hotchkiss took over Jones Manufacturing the Star continued to be made under the Hotchkiss name. Within several years (and after a number of improvements) the Star Fastener evolved to become the Hotchkiss No 1.

COMPO MANUFACTURING & SALES COMPANY

"Compo - It will not clog." So was the slogan when the Compo Sales Company first introduced its new stapler, the Compo, in 1921. Compo Sales Company only ever released the one stapler, although with variants in manufacture and markings. The last known advertisement for the Compo Fastener was in 1927.

Right around this time the Compo Sales Company was acquired by E.H. Hotchkiss Co and with the No. 1 still one of their mainstays even after all these years killed the Compo Fastener. However, by the mid-1930's Compo made a comeback but this time with what were essentially variants of rebranded Hotchkiss staplers.

COMPO MANUFACTURING & SALES COMPANY FASTENERS

No 1C

The No 1C weighs 1.5 pounds and measures 5.25 inches long by 2 inches wide by 4.3125 inches tall. The body, base, and plunger were made of a zinc compound while some of the internal parts were steel. Uses standard staples. Modeled after Hotchkiss models 3A and 3C. This is a well-built, heavy-duty small stapler but is rare.

No 3C
Nickel-plated

The model 3C weighs 1 pound and measures 4.4375 inches long by 1.75 inches wide by 3.5 inches tall. It was made of a zinc alloy with some internal steel parts. The magazine has a capacity of approximately 70 standard staples. Available in the 1930's. this is a rare stapler.

No 3C-54
Nickel-plated

Similar in design to the No 3C except this model uses 0.25 inch crown staples available as Hotchkiss H.54, Compo C.54, or Star 54 staples. Weighs 1 pound and measures 4.4375 inches long by 1.75 inches wide by 3.3125 inches tall. Manufactured using a zinc alloy with some internal steel parts. Available in the 1930's for a short period. This is a rare stapler.

No 4C
Nickel-plated

This fastener is a copy of the Hotchkiss model 1A. It was likely available in the 1930's and perhaps longer. Weighing in at 1 pound 15 ounces and measuring 7.25 inches long by 2 inches wide by 4 inches tall this is every bit as well-made as any of the Hotchkiss staplers. It can hold up to 210 standard size staples in the staple guide. This model stapler is rare.

No 5C
Black hammerloid enamel body and base with chrome plunger only

This is a clone of the Hotchkiss 5A with the only discernible difference being that it has "COMPO" inscribed in large letters on the top part of the base instead of "Hotchkiss". Like the Hotchkiss 5A this is marked "No 5" on the forward part of the base. It is unknown if, like Hotchkiss, Compo sold this as the No 5A, 5C, or if it sold as the No 5. Without corroborating evidence the decision is to call it the 5C to keep in line with other Compo stapler naming conventions. This measures 7.25 inches long by 2 inches wide by 4 inches tall. It weighs 1 pound 8 ounces empty. It can hold up to 210 standard size staples in the staple guide. The No 5A would have been available from the mid-1930's through the 1940's. While the Hotchkiss and Star versions of this model are relatively common, the Compo 5A is a rare stapler seldom seen in the wild.

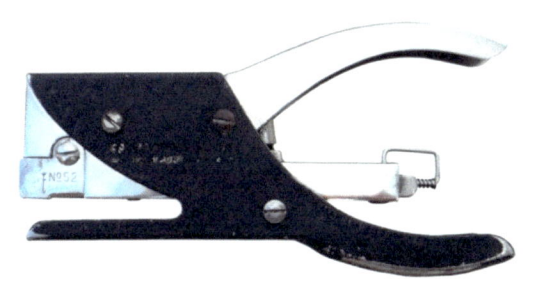

No 52
Chrome with black hammerloid enamel

Similar in most respects to the Hotchkiss No 52. This was available at least in the 1940's, but exact years are impossible to determine. The No 52 used H.52 or Star 54 staples which had a 0.25 inch crown. The magazine could hold up to 70 staples at a time. This fastener weighs 8 ounces and measures 5.75 inches long by .5 inches wide by 2.9375 tall. This model is made from all-steel. Build quality is indistinguishable from the Hotchkiss.

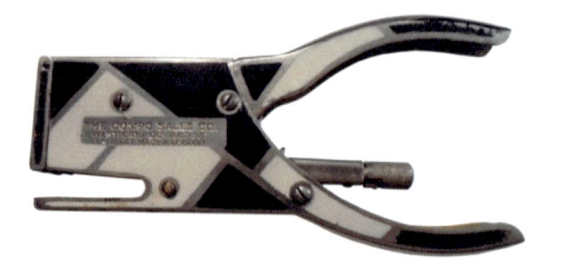

No 54
Chrome with white and black enamel in geometric pattern

Made in Germany the No 54 was a lightweight plier-type stapler that was up for some heavy-duty work. Using no 54 staples (H.54, C.54, or Star 54) it could hold 50 staples at a time. This stapler was very well-built and though the tiny staples were a limiting factor in how it could be used you could say that it "pulled above its weight". Like its Hotchkiss siblings it weighs 6 ounces 5.75 inches long by .5 inches wide by 2.75 inches high. Also like its Hotchkiss siblings the enamel is poor quality and wears off easily. This fastener would have been made in the same timeframe as the Hotchkiss No 54 in the mid-1930's, but unlikely available after 1940. Both Hotchkiss and Star offered four different color schemes for the No 54 and it is likely that all four were released under the Compo name as well. This stapler is rare, rarer even than the Hotchkiss No 54.

Compo
Version 1, original model

Introduced in 1921 and sold through 1922, the original model Compo paper fastener was serious competition for the Hotchkiss No 1. While the contemporary model of the Hotchkiss No 1 was made of a zinc alloy the Compo was made from 100% nickel-plated pressed steel. It used staple strips and was purposely designed so that Hotchkiss No 1 strip staples could be used along with Compo's own "No 1" strip staples. This is a rare fastener.

Compo
Version 2, original model

Cosmetically, version 2 of the Compo is nearly identical to the first version. There is a restyled plunger spring plate but the biggest change is that the body of version 2 is now made from a zinc alloy instead of steel like the previous version. This would have been available approximately 1922-1923. Out of the five versions of this fastener, this is the rarest.

Compo
Version 3, original model

Again, version 3 is nearly identical to the first two versions. Essentially the only difference to version 2 is the addition of the words "PAT. JAN 9,23-OTHERS PEND." etched on the raised bar on the logo between the words Compo and Westport. This was available from 1923 until 1924 or 1925.

Compo
Version 4, original model

Version 4 of the Compo was introduced around 1924/1925 and sold until 1927. It weighs 1 pound 4 ounces empty and measures 4.25 inches long by 2 inches wide by 4.125 inches tall. There are a number of differences between versions 3 and 4. These differences include a smaller "tombstone" logo on the version 4, the logo on the version 4 is now in an indented area. On the left side of version 3 is a panel that can be unscrewed to give you access for repairs, on version 4 this panel is no longer there. And the base is now also made from zinc. This is an uncommon fastener but one that shows up regularly for sale.

Compo
Version 5, original model

There isn't much information on this particular model, but my opinion is that it was available no earlier than 1926 and possibly not until 1927. There are a number of changes between the version 4 above and this version. While the "tombstone" logo is the same size it now contains information for A.H. Irvin Company. Note that the plunger is larger and more rounded. The plunger spring plate has been totally removed from this model. There is also a new feature. If you look towards the rear *you'll see a small lever. This is a staple release lever which wasn't a feature on the previous versions. The body and base are still made of a zinc alloy. This is a very rare fastener.*

STAR PAPER FASTENER COMPANY INC.

The Star Paper Fastener Company Inc., from its very inception, sold rebranded Hotchkiss staplers. What E.H. Hotchkiss seems to have done is to release many, if not all, of its stapler models rebranded as Compo and Star Paper Fasteners. However, when Star first started it also released a series of plier-type staplers based on the same patents that Neva-Clog staplers were based on.

Star Paper Fasteners were first seen around 1928 and were sold at least through the 1950's and likely until E.H. Hotchkiss was acquired by Vail Manufacturing.

*NOTE: The models in this section are in numerical order without regard to any preceding letters. For example, model S12 will precede model 15. It is likely that all Star stapling machine model numbers were preceded by an "S" but this has only been proven for some models. For those models where it is unproven if their model number was preceded by an "S" it has been left off.

STAR PAPER FASTENER COMPANY INC. FASTENERS

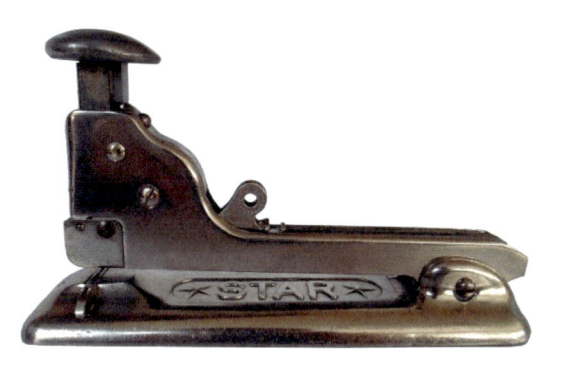

No S5

Version 1, chrome

The model S5 weighs 1 pound 7 ounces and measures 7.4375 inches long by 2 inches wide by 4.125 tall. The magazine held a strip of 210 standard size staples. This fastener was introduced about 1936 and likely available through the mid-1940's. It's a common fastener to find in this finish. Like others I've mentioned the Star S5 is well-built and since it uses standard staples makes a wonderful addition to your vintage desk.

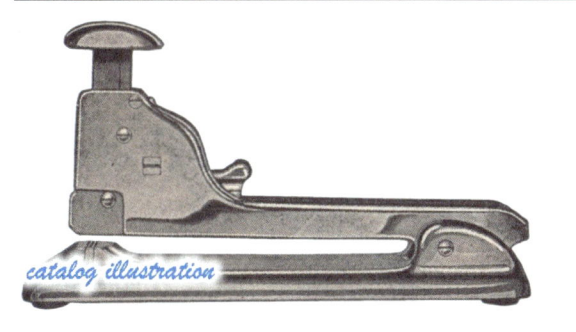

No S5

Version 1, black hammerloid enamel with chrome plunger and base

The Star Paper Fastener Company didn't seem bound to using the same model numbers as their Hotchkiss counterparts. This is a clone of the Hotchkiss 5A with the only discernible difference being that it has "STAR" inscribed in large letters on the top part of the base instead of "Hotchkiss". Like the Hotchkiss 5A this is marked "No 5" on the forward part of the base.

No S6
Chrome with black hammerloid enamel.

The model S6 weighs 1 pound and measures 5.5 inches long by 2 inches wide by 4.125 inches tall. It holds 105 standard size staples at one time. It was available by 1940 and sold through the mid-1950's. You see this version less often than the Hotchkiss No 6A making this an uncommon fastener.

No S6
Black hammerloid enamel body and base with chrome plunger only.

The No S6 had a sliding anvil and it could form permanent or temporary staples. It could also be used as a tacker in which form it excelled. You see these about as often as the Hotchkiss No 6A making this an uncommon fastener.

No S6
Chrome

Note that this version of the model S6 the model number is not marked on the front of the base. All versions of the Star model S6 are less common than the Hotchkiss models. This is an uncommon fastener.

No 10 Automatic Tacker

The No 10 was sold in the late 1930's and likely through the 1950's like its Hotchkiss cousin. This tacker measures 5.75 inches tall by 6.25 inches long by .95 inches wide and weighs 1 pound 12 ounces. It uses No 1 strip staples and holds 50 in its magazine. This is a rare fastener in any condition.

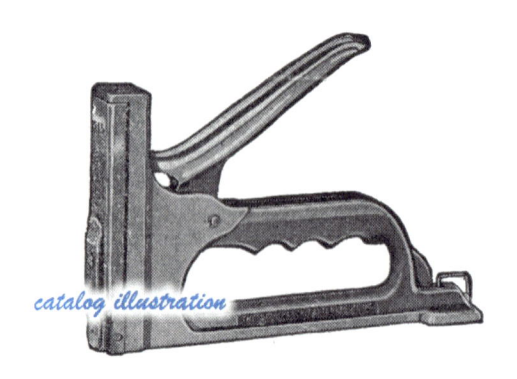

No S12 Tacker

The No S12 was designed for light construction and home maintenance tasks. It was advertised mostly to commercial businesses for putting up signage in places where you couldn't use a hammer. It uses special heavy-duty staples. It measures 7.5 inches long by 5.25 inches tall and weighs 1 pound 13 ounces.

No S-15 Tacker
Polished metal

The Star S-15 Tacker weighs 1 pound 14 ounces empty and measures 7.5 inches long by 1.5 inches wide by 5.125 inches tall. The operating handle, front plate, and internal parts are made of steel. The remainder of the tacker is made from a zinc alloy. Uses staples with a .53125 (17/32) inch crown, 0.25 inch leg, and a wire size of .025 max.

No S-18 Tacker
Polished steel with grey enamel

The No S-18 was designed for light construction and home maintenance tasks. It uses special industrial-grade heavy-duty staples. It measures 7.5 inches long by 5.25 inches tall and weighs 1 pound 13 ounces.

No '31 Wire Stapler
Nickel-plated

The No '31 weighs 2 pounds and measures 7.25 inches long by 2 inches wide by 4.375 inches tall. This has a capacity of 210 staples. It also has a ruler built in to the base. While you won't see this fastener quite as often as it's Hotchkiss cousins it is nevertheless a common stapler.

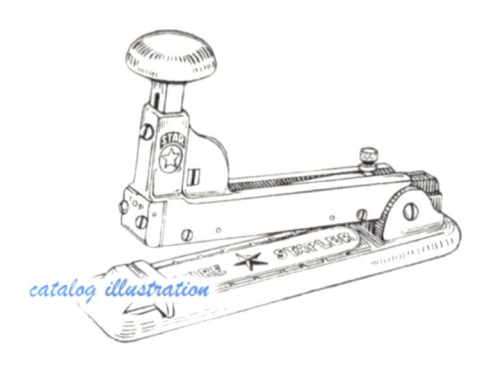

No '31 Wire Stapler
black hammerloid with chrome plunger

catalog illustration

While the Hotchkiss 1A was introduced in 1927, I'm going to go out on a limb and state that "The New '31 Star Non-Clogging Paper Fastener" was introduced in 1931. The black hammerloid version probably was introduced several years later in the mid-1930's. This stapler is a clone of the Hotchkiss model 1A and just like its cousin is built like a tank. Both the nickel-plated and black hammerloid versions of this fastener are great staplers that use standard size staples making them perfect for your vintage desk. The '31 in this finish is seen less often and is an uncommon stapler to find in the wild.

Hotchkiss No 1A / Star No '31
Black hammerloid enamel body and base with copper plated plunger, block, screws

This is likely a one-off hybrid of a Hotchkiss 1A body on a Star '31 base. However, it shows that these models existed in copper plate. Furthermore, the wear patterns show that this pairing were together from the very beginning, possibly even from the factory. This is the only copper plated fastener of any kind seen for Hotchkiss, Star or Compo making this an exceptionally rare piece.

No '31 Tacker
Nickel-plated

While most desktop staplers can be used as a tacker, the more popular staplers often were modified and released as specialty tackers. This configuration is a pattern tacker stapler. The handle is a zinc alloy in black hammerloid enamel and is custom configured to this model. The handle makes it a bit taller and longer than a standard '31 but it is at heart a No '31.

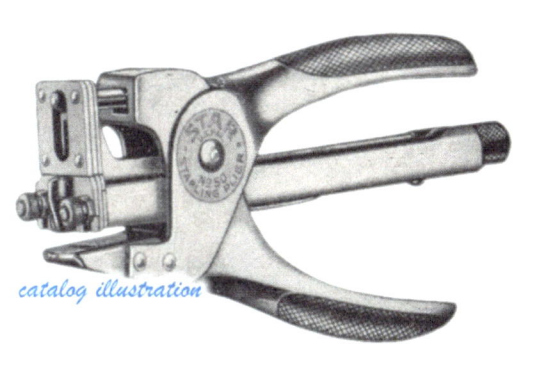

No 50 Stapling Plier
Nickel-plated

catalog illustration

The No 50 Stapling Plier weighs 8 ounces and holds 50 staples in its magazine. It takes proprietary staples that have a crown size of 11mm which correspond to Neva-Clog A1000 and L1000 staples. This isn't a coincidence. This fastener was made in Germany and the patent(s) covering this fastener would have belonged to Max Vogel, the owner of Neva-Clog in the U.S. and M. Vogel A.G. in Germany. This fastener was likely produced by M. Vogel A.G. or possibly by Elastic A.G. which was the successor company to M. Vogel A.G. This fastener would have been produced from approximately 1931 until the mid-to-late 1930's. This is a very rare fastener.

No 51 Stapling Plier
Nickel-plated

The No 51 Stapling Plier weighs 1 pound and measures 7.375 inches long by 1.125 inches wide by 3.75 inches tall. It holds 100 staples of the same size as the No 50 Plier. The staples it uses have an 11mm crown and the Neva-Clog A1000 and L1000 staples would fit in this perfectly. Star sold staples for this, and other, fasteners as Star 51 staples. This fastener was made in Germany and the patent(s) involved would have belonged to Max Vogel. Both the models 50 and 51 would have been manufactured at the same time, by the same manufacturer, and in the same factory. In 1936 Neva-Clog introduced the model S100 plier stapler and this is likely when Star stopped selling both models 50 and 51. This is a very rare fastener.

No 52
Chrome

Available in the mid 1930's, this stapler was likely available as long as the Hotchkiss No 52 was. This fastener weighs 8 ounces and measures 5.75 inches long by .5 inches wide by 2.8125 tall. The No 52 was a light-duty stapler that used the very small H.52 or Star 54 staples. As such its usefulness was mostly in homes and schools. This is a rare stapler and much more difficult to find than the Hotchkiss No 52.

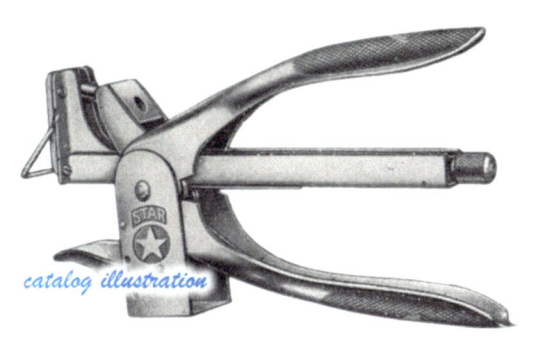

No 52 Plier Fastener
Nickel-plated

catalog illustration

The Star No 52 Plier Type Fastener is a combination fastening and tacking device. It has an adjustable jaw which can be spread to 1.125 inches by removing an "adjusting pin", dropping the lower jaw to the last hole and inserting the pin to hold it securely. Then the plier has become a tacker. Removing the pin and raising the lower jaw to a top position makes it a paper fastener. Attached to the front is a wire gauge. For temporary tacking you pull this to the lowest position underneath the magazine bar where it makes a clearance between the top of the staple and the wood. When the wire gauge is in the position shown in the illustration the staple will be driven flush to the wood. This model uses Star 51 staples with either a 0.25 inch leg or 0.375 inch leg. The No 52 was made in Germany and is a very rare stapler.

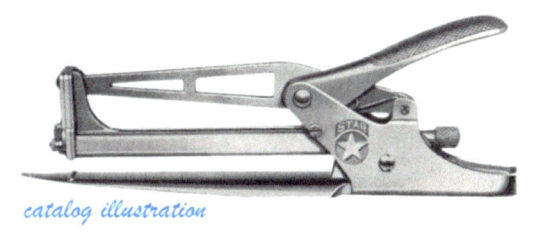

No 53 Plier Fastener
Nickel-plated

catalog illustration

According to sales brochures the No 53 Plier Type Fastener was designed to be used where merchandise to be ticketed or fastened cannot be brought to the machine or where a clearance of five inches is needed for stapling purposes. A simple leverage arrangement enables the device to be easily operated with one hand while the other hand holds the material to be ticketed or stapled. This fastener uses the Star 51 staples. This model has never actually been spotted in the wild nor has even a picture been seen. This is an extremely rare model.

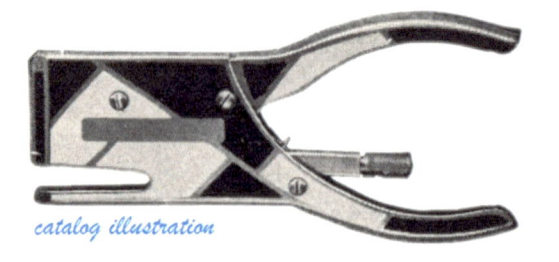

No 54
Nickel with white and black enamel in geometric pattern

catalog illustration

Designed and manufactured in Germany, these highly decorative plier-type staplers were well-built and a pleasure to use. While this fastener was sold under the Hotchkiss, Compo, and Star names they were all the exact same fastener.

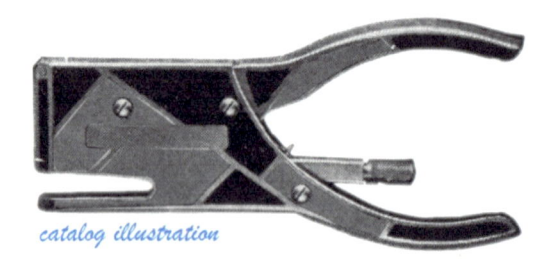

No 54
Nickel with red and black enamel in geometric pattern

catalog illustration

The No 54 Plier Staplers are essentially rebranded Elastic Juwels which also sported similar (but different) geometric enamels in similar colors. The paint used on these isn't very durable and is easily scratched and worn.

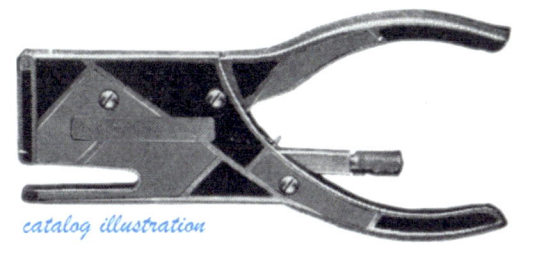

No 54
Nickel with green and black enamel in geometric pattern

catalog illustration

The No 54 measures 5.75 inches long by .5 inches wide by 2.75 inches high and weighs 6 ounces empty. All versions of the Star No 54 should be considered rare.

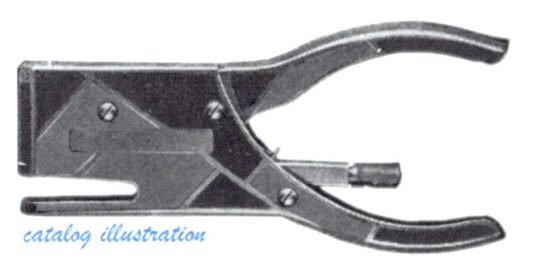

No 54
Nickel with orange and yellow enamel in geometric pattern

catalog illustration

The No 54 used very small staples and held 50 in the magazine. These were available as the Hotchkiss H.54, Compo C.54, and the Star 54. Staples made for the Elastic Juwel will fit in these.

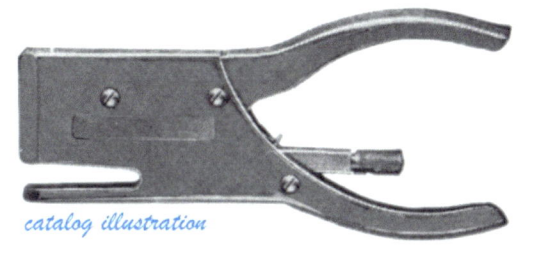

No 54
Nickel-plated

catalog illustration

This fastener would have been made in the same timeframe as the Hotchkiss and Compo No 54 in the mid-1930's, but unlikely available after 1940. This stapler is rarer than both the Hotchkiss and Compo No 54.

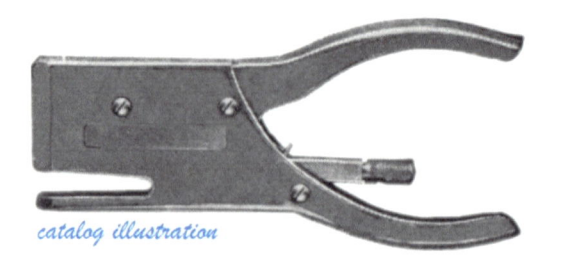

No 54
Cadmium finish

catalog illustration

Cadmium plating isn't a finish seen often. It does have some advantages over Nickel such as higher corrosion resistance. In businesses where the fastener might be exposed to salt or harsh chemicals then this would be a superior choice. Cadmium-plating isn't as shiny as nickel and tends to have a very slight bluish tint. Cadmium is also a highly toxic metal. While plated items are safe enough the plating process can be environmentally unfriendly. It is unknown if Compo or Hotchkiss had this as an option.

No S101 Zephyr
Nickel with black hammerloid enamel

The Star Zephyr is a rare stapler that is also very desirable. The only difference between the models S101 and 101A is on the bottom of the base one has Star Paper Fastener Co inscribed and the other has the Hotchkiss Sales Co. This measures 8 inches long by 2.125 inches wide by 3.25 inches high and weighs 1 pound 10 ounces empty. The magazine holds 210 standard-size staples at a time in a front loading carrier. This fastener (along with the Hotchkiss 101A) came with what was called the "quadri-clinch anvil". The anvil could be turned to give you one of four different fastenings: temporary, pinning, light duty, and permanent. The light duty setting was a standard clinch while the permanent setting was actually an extra flat clinch.

The Zephyr was available from office suppliers from approximately 1940 until about 1946.

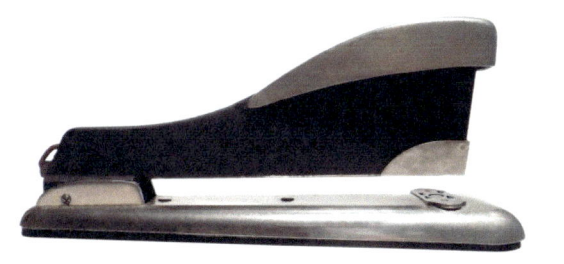

No 120
Chrome with black hammerloid enamel

The model 120 weighs 1 pound 6 ounces and measures 8 inches long by 2.15 inches wide by 3.4 inches tall. This holds a full strip of 210 staples. This was originally available in the mid-1930's through the 1940's. Like many of the Star Fastener variants it is a rare stapler.

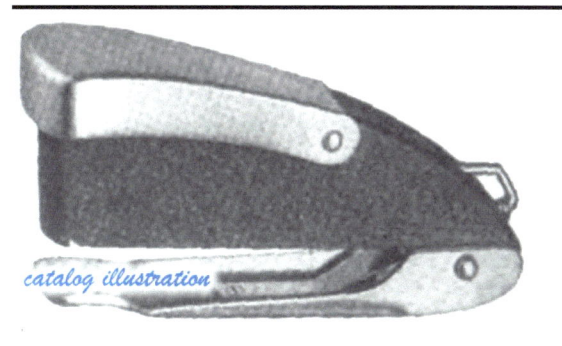

No 122P Plier
Nickel with black hammerloid enamel

catalog illustration

The No 122P weighs 8 ounces and measures 4.25 inches long by 1 inch wide by 2.5 inches tall. Holds 105 standard size staples. This is a rare stapler.

Comet Tacker
Chrome with grey hammerloid enamel

The Comet was designed for light construction and home maintenance tasks. It uses special industrial-grade heavy-duty staples sold as Comet Staples. It measures 7.5 inches long by 5.25 inches tall and weighs 1 pound 13 ounces. This is an uncommon fastener and one that is difficult to find in good condition because of its use in construction.

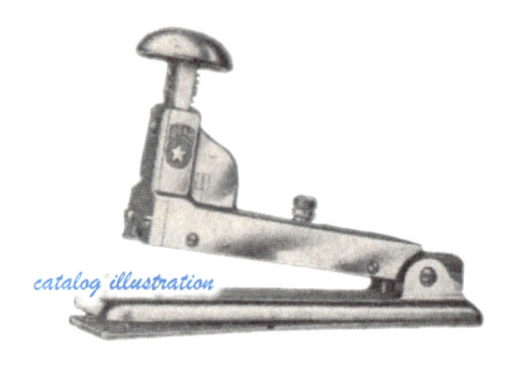

catalog illustration

Mechanical Anvil Machine
Nickel-plated

The Star Mechanical Anvil is a flat-stitch staple machine. If you look at the illustration note how the bottom seems to be peeling off. At the forward end (where it seems to be peeling) there are actually two springs that are underneath the anvil and attached to another base. Essentially, there is the main base and a secondary base underneath that. Available in the early 1930's. This is an extremely rare machine.

Model "O" Fastener
Nickel-plated

The Star Model "O" weighs 1 pound and measures 4.5 inches long by 1.25 inches wide by 3.375 inches tall. It holds 50 staples of H.54, C.54, or Star 54 staples. This fastener is the same as the 3C-54 from Compo and Hotchkiss and like them the Model "O" is rare and a difficult stapler to find.

Model SN Fastener
Nickel-plated

catalog illustration

The Star Model SN Fastener does two things at once. It not only staples but will punch a hole in the material being stapled. This stapler was designed for merchants who sold small goods in plastic bags. The stapler allowed the merchant to staple a folded card on the top of the bag and also place a hole in this card so that it could then be hung on a display. This type of fastener would be impractical in a factory setting but in a small store or similar setting would be extremely effective. Like many of the Star specialty fasteners this was not made in great quantities and is a rare item.

STAPLER ANATOMY

It's important to know the language of collecting staplers and that starts with knowing the names of the different parts. Below are the two most common types of staplers offered by Hotchkiss/Compo/Star; the desk-type and the plier-type . The charts below show the basic parts of all staplers of that type.

DESKTOP STAPLER

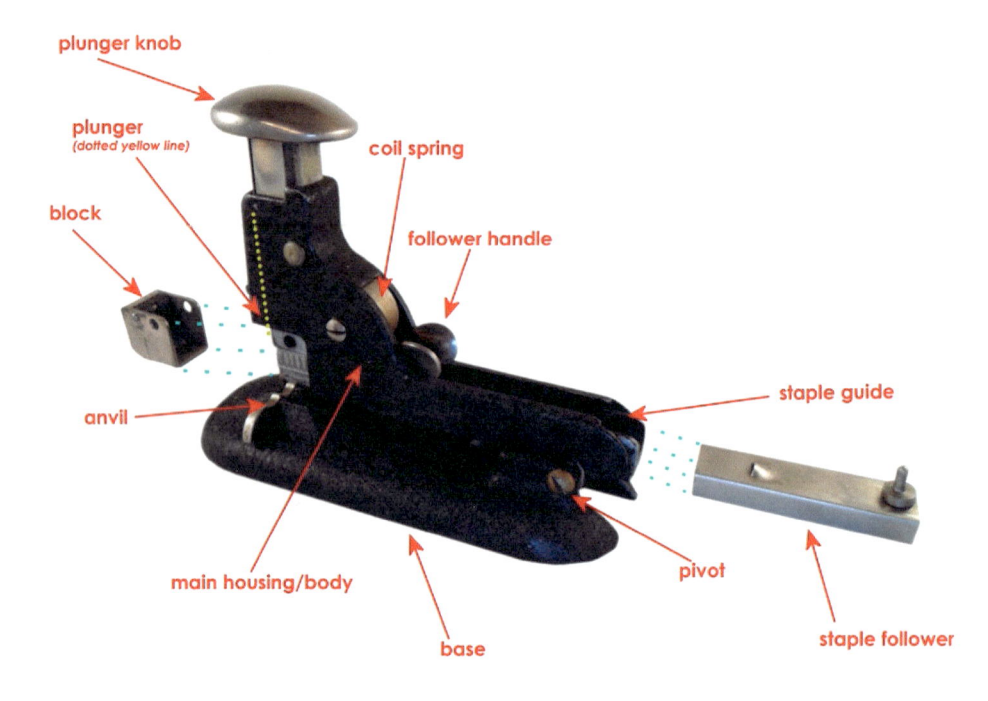

While there are many different types of staplers, the form shown above was the main office/desk type fastener through the 1950's. The Star Paper Fastener by the Jones Manufacturing Company used this form for their revolutionary design although the internal mechanics were different due to using strip staples. Staplers of this type are still manufactured but mostly by European companies.

PLIER-TYPE STAPLER

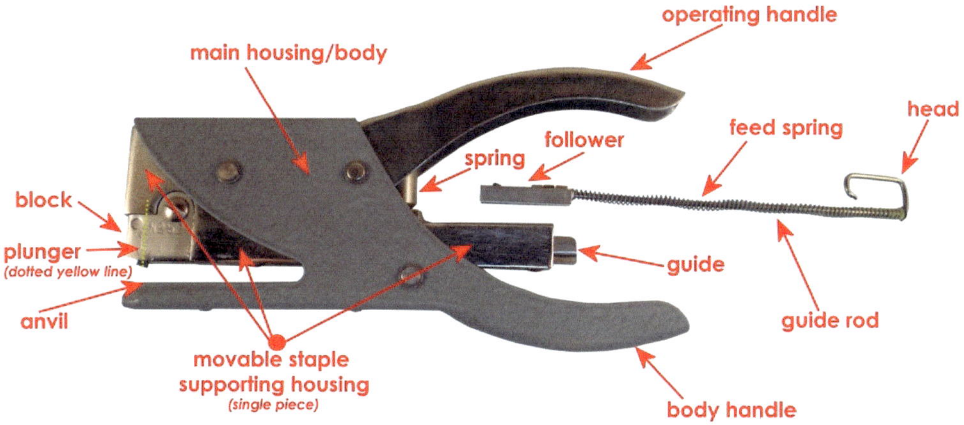

operating handle
main housing/body
head
feed spring
follower
spring
block
plunger
(dotted yellow line)
guide
anvil
guide rod
movable staple
supporting housing
(single piece)
body handle

The plier-type stapler did not see widespread use in offices but instead was mostly used in commercial and shipping settings. The advantage of this form is the ability to take the stapler to the item to be stapled making it totally portable. With a desktop stapler you bring the paper to the stapler, with a plier-type you bring the stapler to the paper. The main limitation of this type is that it could not be used for heavy-duty stapling like the desktop version could.

STAPLE REMOVERS

Hotchkiss staple remover. These came in red, green, black, blue, and tan. They were designed to remove modern office staples.

STAPLE ANATOMY

KNOW YOUR MODERN STAPLES!

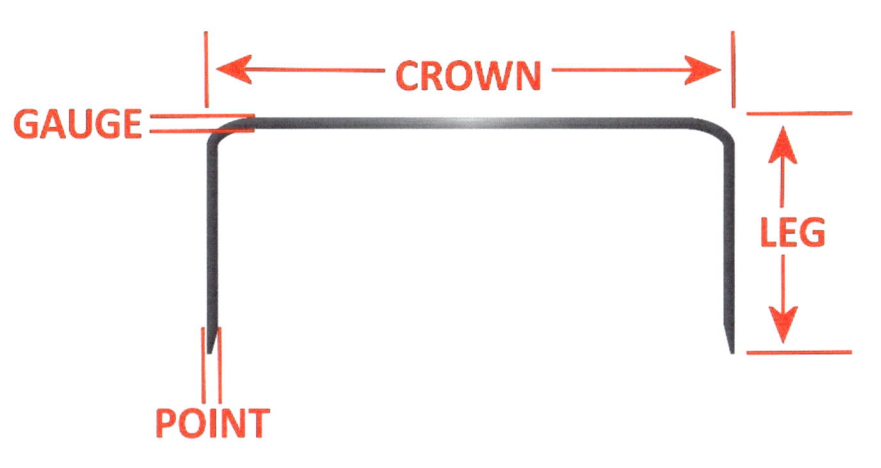

There are three main things to know about a staple:

1) Crown Size - In the U.S. this is expressed in inches. In Europe and most other places it will be expressed in millimeters. The crown size for a standard staple is .5 inches or 12.8mm.

2) Leg Size - as with crown, this is expressed in either inches or millimeters. However, you are just as likely to see it in millimeters in the U.S. as you are in inches. The leg size on a standard staple is usually .25 inches or 6mm but can be slightly longer or shorter. Leg size is especially important in industrial staplers.

3) Gauge - this is the thickness of the wire used in the staple. The higher the gauge, the thinner the wire. You oftentimes won't see gauge mentioned on U.S. staples, but the standard is 26 gauge in both the U.S. and in Europe. Most Hotchkiss staples gave the gauge as decimal parts of an inch, i.e. wire size .025. In this example .025 thickness converts to 24 gauge. And because you wouldn't want this to be simple, the larger the wire size the thicker the wire. Or it can be stated as the lower the gauge the larger the wire size. Noted earlier is that 26 gauge is considered standard. This converts to .019 wire size.

For Hotchkiss, you'll never see metric sizes given. You're also unlikely to see crown sizes given. Hotchkiss staples were labeled either "standard" or used the fastener model number, i.e. No 52 staples. You will, however, see leg size given for some staples. For instance, you have the No 52 3-16 staples. This meant the leg was 3/16 of an inch.

4) Point - this is the way the end of the leg is cut. By far the most used is chisel point, but you'll see others such as blunt and divergent.

STAPLE CLINCHING

There are essentially five different ways that a stapler can clinch a staple.

1. Permanent

Sometimes called "standard", this is the way most every stapler fastens papers together. The legs of the staple are simply bent back towards the paper in the direction of the center of the staple crown. In order to remove the staple it will need to be pried off.

2. Pinning

Most people don't even realize that almost all staplers made today have two staple settings; permanent and pin. Pinning is meant to be a temporary way to fasten papers. You pin your papers with your stapler, and when you want to remove this staple all you will need to do is slide it out. This setting is great when working with clothing also.

3. Tacking

Tacking is used if you wish to hang something on a wall, such as a special notice or a poster. In this arrangement the staple effectively becomes two nails connected by a horizontal bar. Most modern staplers can be used as a tacker simply by rotating the base 180 degrees to the rear.

4. Temporary

This is a variation of pinning where one leg is folded inward and the other outward. To remove, simply slide the staple in the direction of the inward folded leg.

5. Flat Clinch

The flat clinch is a variation of the permanent clinch. The "flat" in flat clinch is in reference to how the legs are folded, not the crown. A flat clinch is useful when stacking or filing lots of fastened groups of papers as it allows them to be stacked/filed without that one corner of the pile that quickly rises much higher than the other three corners.

STAPLES

STRIP STAPLES

Above is a picture of a Hotchkiss staple strip. The tell is that on each end there is a small T-shaped tab. A staple-strip looks similar to today's magazine staples. The difference is that a staple-strip was actually formed and cut from a single piece of metal. When stapling, you pressed down on the stapler plunger and it cut the staple from the strip. This necessitated a certain amount of force that today would be considered excessive. As a matter of fact, it was not unheard of when these were popular for office workers to have a rubber mallet nearby to use with this. If you've ever wondered why the plunger top of a Hotchkiss No 1 is all beat up this is likely the reason.

Another item to note is that staple strips were not manufactured to the same tolerances that you see today. It was not unusual for the crown or leg of a strip of staples to differ by as much as an eighth of an inch from box to box.

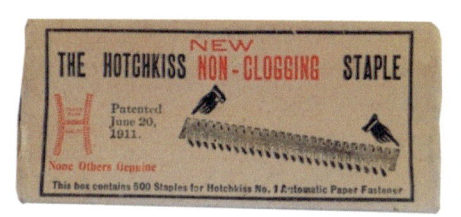

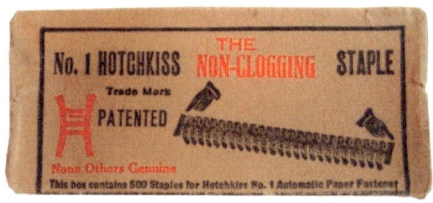

Staples for the Hotchkiss No 1. In order for a strip stapler to load a strip of staples and make it ready to fasten, it had to feed the strip into position by running a staple through the plunger. This meant the first staple in a strip was always wasted.

Hotchkiss eventually solved this by adding that special "T" tab at each end. The tab was designed so that it could be run through the stapler and position the strip for use. When the tab was first introduced the box was labeled "New Non-Clogging" but as time went by it was changed to read "The Non-Clogging" staple. Older versions of the No 1 staple did not have this tab. While I would never recommend using an antique stapler, if you must then I always recommend you use staples made by the same company that made the fastener to reduce the chance of issues. The crown size is 0.375 (3/8) inches. The leg is 0.1875 (3/16) inches. The strip is 3.4375 (3-7/16) inches long.

Compo staples were high quality strip staples but without any special tabs or such. They were sold for the original Compo fastener but ads always mentioned that they fit "other standard staple machines". It wasn't an accident that the original Compo was designed to use staples of exactly the same size as the Hotchkiss No 1. Even if you didn't purchase the Compo fastener they hoped you'd buy their staples which were less expensive than the Hotchkiss branded ones. The crown size is 0.375 (3/8) inch. The leg is 0.21875 (7/32) inches. The strip is 3.125 (3-1/8) inches long.

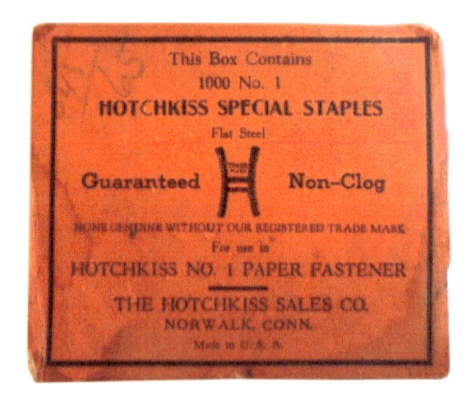

A box containing a larger amount of Hotchkiss No 1 staples. Note that it does not state these are the "new non-clogging" staples so it is the original style without the end tabs. The crown size is 0.375 (3/8) inches. The leg is 0.1875 (3/16) inches. The strip is 3.125 (3-1/8) inches long.

Another box of 1000 Hotchkiss No 1 staples. Note that this is for use in both the Hotchkiss No 1 and the Unit fasteners. That dates this box to on or after 1922. While it states "Guaranteed Non-Clog" it does not state "New Non-Clogging". That makes these the original style without the end tabs. The crown size is 0.375 (3/8) inches. The leg is 0.21 (7/32) inches. The strip is 3.125 (3-1/8) inches long.

Hotchkiss did manufacture their staples for other resellers to sell under their own name, and National Office Supply Company was one of those resellers. Despite the box, these are genuine Hotchkiss staples and it so states on the box sides. This box holds strips for the Hotchkiss No 1. The crown size is 0.375 (3/8) inches. The leg is 0.21875 (7/32) inches. The strip is 3.4375 (3-7/16) inches long.

84

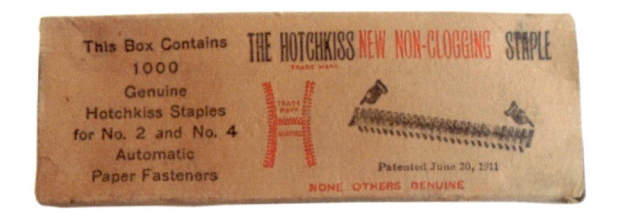

Staples for the No 2 and No 4 Hotchkiss machines. The legs were longer on these staples than on the No 1 allowing them to hold more papers. The staple strips were also longer. Crown size is 0.375 (3/8) inch. The leg size is 0.28125 (9/32) long. The strip is 5.25 (5-1/4) inches long.

Staple strips for the Hotchkiss No 3 stapling machine. Both the crown and legs are longer than the other types of Hotchkiss staples. The crown is 0.5 (1/2) inch. The leg is 0.28125 (9/32) inches long. The strip is 5.6875 (5-11/16) inches long.

MODERN STAPLES

When people talk about staples, this is what they usually picture - the modern staple. This is a picture of actual Hotchkiss standard size staples. Despite the box that they came from being at least 60 years old they can still be used in any stapler that uses standard size staples - including any stapler being sold today. Different size modern staples (e.g. the Hotchkiss 52) will look identical to these and you wouldn't notice the difference unless you saw them side-by-side.

- made specifically for the model 15 Comet Tacker
- available in 0.1875 (3/16) and 0.25 (1/4) inch leg lengths
- wire size of 0.025 inch

- made specifically for the model S-18 Tacker
- available in 0.1875 (3/16) and 0.25 (1/4) inch leg lengths
- wire size of 0.025 inch

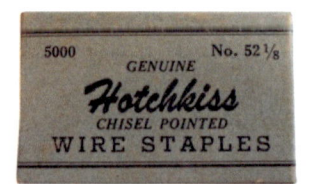

- 0.25 (1/4) inch crown and 0.125 (1/8) inch leg
- fits Hotchkiss/Compo/Star No 52 and 54 plier stapler, Hotchkiss/Compo No 3C-54, Hotchkiss 3A-54, and Star Model "O"

- 0.25 (1/4) inch crown and 0.1875 (3/16) inch leg
- fits Hotchkiss/Compo/Star No 52 and 54 plier stapler, Hotchkiss/Compo No 3C-54, Hotchkiss 3A-54, and Star Model "O"

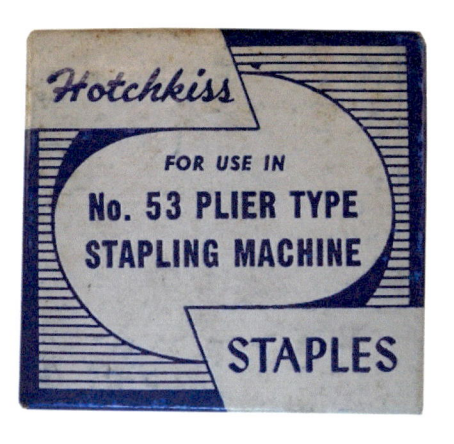

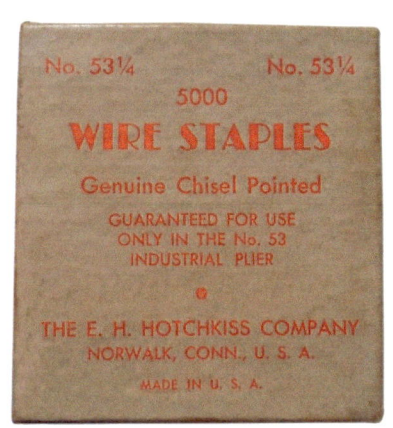

- made specifically for the model 53 plier stapler
- crown size of 0.4375 (7/16) inch
- available in 0.3125 (5/16) and 0.25 (1/4) inch leg lengths
- wire size of 0.019 inch

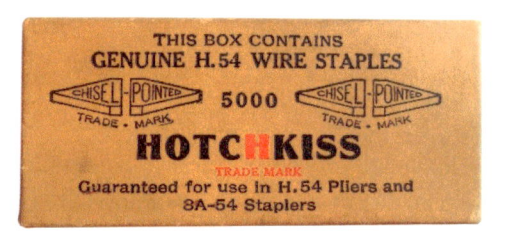

- 0.25 (1/4) inch crown and 0.15625 (5/32) inch leg
- fits Hotchkiss/Compo/Star No 52 and 54 plier stapler, Hotchkiss/Compo No 3C-54, Hotchkiss 3A-54, and Star Model "O"

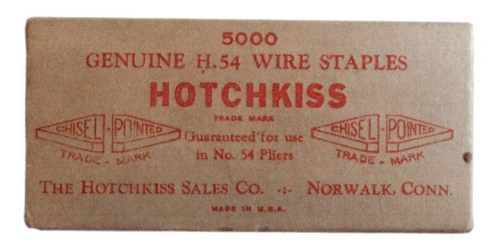

- 0.25 (1/4) inch crown and 0.15625 (5/32) inch leg

- fits Hotchkiss/Compo/Star No 52 and 54 plier stapler, Hotchkiss/Compo No 3C-54, Hotchkiss 3A-54, and Star Model "O"

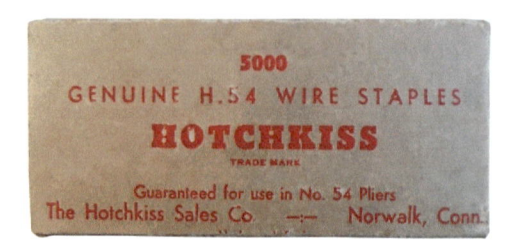

- 0.25 (1/4) inch crown and 0.15625 (5/32) inch leg
- fits Hotchkiss/Compo/Star No 52 and 54 plier stapler, Hotchkiss/Compo No 3C-54, Hotchkiss 3A-54, and Star Model "O"

- 0.25 (1/4) inch crown and 0.15625 (5/32) inch leg
- fits Hotchkiss/Compo/Star No 52 and 54 plier stapler, Hotchkiss/Compo No 3C-54, Hotchkiss 3A-54, and Star Model "O"

- 0.25 (1/4) inch crown and 0.15625 (5/32) inch leg
- fits Hotchkiss/Compo/Star No 52 and 54 plier stapler, Hotchkiss/Compo No 3C-54, Hotchkiss 3A-54, and Star Model "O"

- 0.25 (1/4) inch crown and 0.125 (1/8) inch leg
- crown is slightly rounded and legs angle inward at approximately 88 degrees to the plane of the crown
- also known as "Coronet" staples
- fits Hotchkiss No 57 plier stapler but will not fit other staplers that use 1/4 inch crown staples

- 0.5 (1/2) inch crown and 0.25 (1/4) inch leg
- fits the majority of staplers made after 1930 and a number of staplers made prior

- 0.5 (1/2) inch crown and 0.25 (1/4) inch leg
- fits the majority of staplers made after 1930 and a number of staplers made prior

- 0.5 (1/2) inch crown and 0.25 (1/4) inch leg
- fits the majority of staplers made after 1930 and a number of staplers made prior

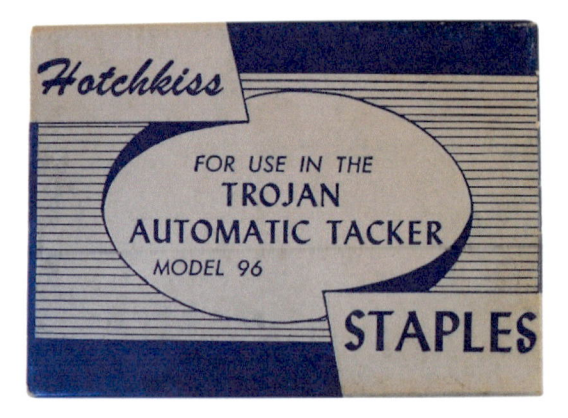

- made specifically for the model D-96 Trojan Tacker
- available in 0.31255 (5/16), 0.375 (3/8), and 0.25 (1/4) inch leg lengths
- wire size of 0.025 inch

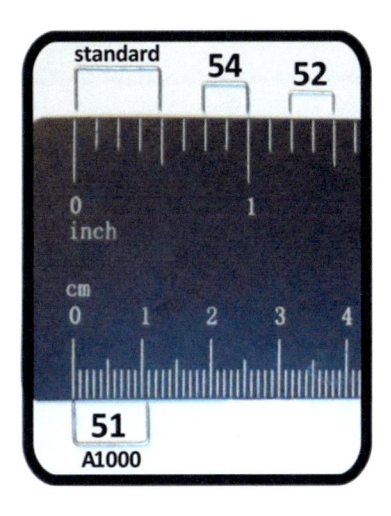

A comparison of the various staples used by Hotchkiss, et al. There is not shown above a sample of a box of Star 51 staples, but note that the 51 has an 11mm crown and corresponds to the Neva-Clog A1000. The 54 and 52 staples have identical crown sizes but the leg sizes available for the 54 were longer than the 52. A standard size staple is twice as wide as the 54 and 52 staple sizes.

ADVERTISEMENTS

1897

The Hotchkiss Automatic Paper Fastener

STYLE No. 1
PRICE $1.50

Complete Catalog on Request

¶ The Hotchkiss No. 1 Automatic Paper Fastener uses a single strip (see cut) on which there are 25 staples. These staples when inserted into the machine are automatically cut off and fed forward, accurately and without failure. The staple is always ready to be driven and a single blow will drive it through 1 to 25 sheets of paper, and with the same movement feed forward the next staple.

ALEX H. IRVIN COMPANY, CURWENSVILLE, PA.

1907

SATURDAY, JULY 19, '13

Hotchkiss Paper Fasteners

1—Uses a single strip of 25 staples, which, when inserted in the machine are automatically cut off and fed forward. The forward staple is always ready to be driven, and a single blow will suffice to drive it through 1 to 25 sheets of paper each. Each....$1.50
Extra staples, 500 in box 25c

Clipless Paper Fasteners

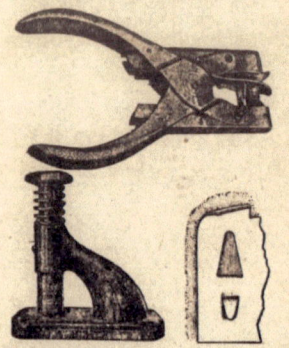

Will fasten from two to ten sheets together without use of metal fasteners of any kind. Made of steel, heavily nickel plated.
1—Hand Press, each $3.00
2—Stand or table press, each $3.50

Hotchkiss Fastener No. 2

2—Made of the very finest tool steel obtainable, every part is acurately made, is strong and durable. Each....$4.00
Extra staples, 500 staples in box........30c

Eyelet Presses and Eyelets
(The Triumph)

Metal, nickel plated, is greatly superior to any of its kind. The "gauge" is a new feature of great utility, and all the obnoxious breakage of springs, etc., which continually accrues in other eyelet punches, is impossible in the Triumph. Each....$1.75

(Regular Eyelets)

B—250 in a box..................20c
DB—Short. 250 in a box..........25c
JN—250 in a box................25c
DB Long. 250 in a box..........50c

Grabbler Check Protector

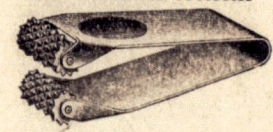

Made of steel, nicely nickeled, heavily embosses the paper by drawing the little rollers across the check. Made to carry in the vest pocket, should be carried by every man who writes checks. Price, each......25c

PATENT NOS. 781,631, 763,503. (COPYRIGHTED).

OWL CLIP

100 IN A BOX   15 CENTS PER BOX   10 BOXES $1.00
Manufactured by
OWL SUPPLY COMPANY
BOSTON, MASS.

The Owl made of steel wire, packed 100 in a box, per box—2, Medium size, 10c 3, Large size, 15

THE KANSAN PRINTING COMPANY---Office Supply Department.

1913

Interesting-and-Important!

OVER twenty-five years of good service have proved nothing wrong with Hotchkiss Automatic Paper Fasteners. The same record is evidence that Hotchkiss Staples are perfect. Any complaint of faulty operation *must* be due to the use of imitation staples.

Investigation establishes this to be actually the case. When a Hotchkiss machine refuses to work properly, when staples clog, jam, or break, it's a safe bet that *imitation staples* are being used.

These imitations are not in line with the feeder guide of Hotchkiss Fasteners. They are made of soft metal, are dull, easily bent and broken—quite incapable of good service in Hotchkiss machines.

The genuine Hotchkiss Staples are perfectly aligned with the feeder. They are made of nickel steel, non-rusting, untarnishable, straight, sharp, strong. Each strip has blank ends so that no Staple is wasted.

For your own best interests carry and recommend only the genuine HOTCHKISS Staples. You will have no dissatisfied customers. You will be building your business on the firm foundation of *good will* and *service!*

Write for Selling Helps.

HOTCHKISS SALES COMPANY
NORWALK.   CONN.

FIVE STYLES
HOTCHKISS
PAPER FASTENERS & TACKING MACHINES

1921

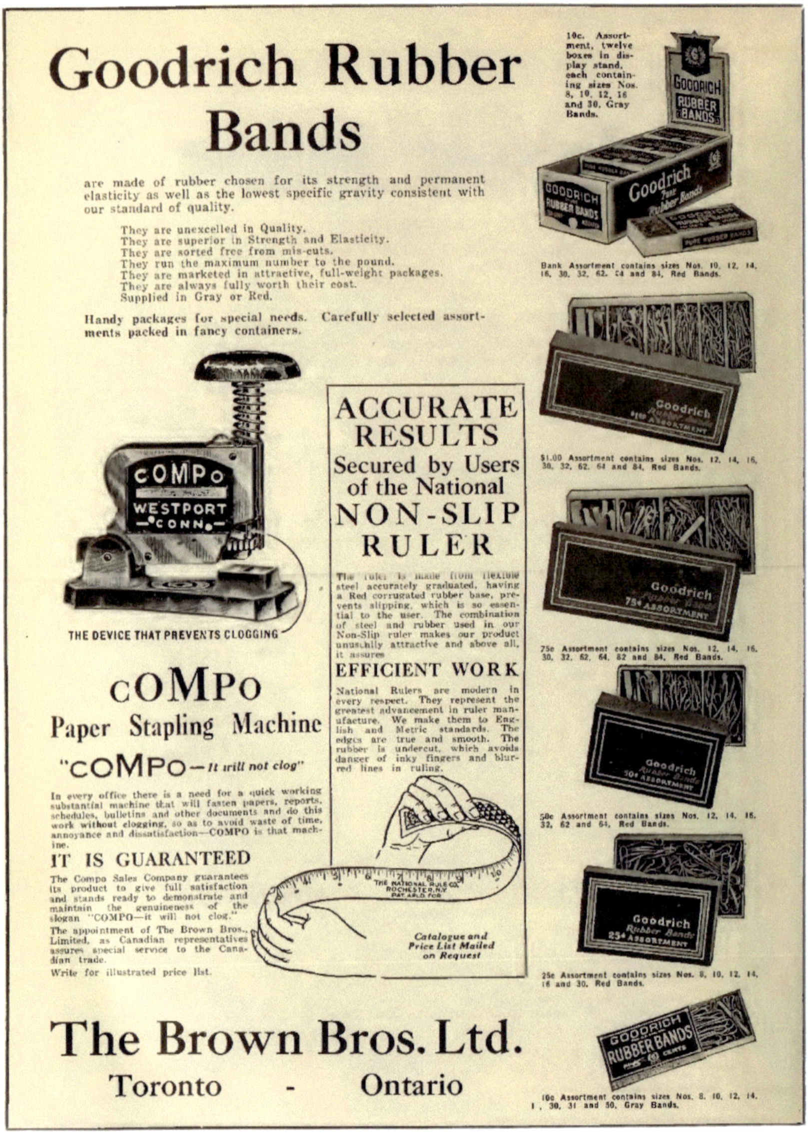

Goodrich Rubber Bands

are made of rubber chosen for its strength and permanent elasticity as well as the lowest specific gravity consistent with our standard of quality.

They are unexcelled in Quality.
They are superior in Strength and Elasticity.
They are sorted free from mis-cuts.
They run the maximum number to the pound.
They are marketed in attractive, full-weight packages.
They are always fully worth their cost.
Supplied in Gray or Red.

Handy packages for special needs. Carefully selected assortments packed in fancy containers.

10c. Assortment, twelve boxes in display stand, each containing sizes Nos. 8, 10, 12, 16 and 30, Gray Bands.

Bank Assortment contains sizes Nos. 10, 12, 14, 16, 30, 32, 62, 64 and 84, Red Bands.

$1.00 Assortment contains sizes Nos. 12, 14, 16, 30, 32, 62, 64 and 84, Red Bands.

75c Assortment contains sizes Nos. 12, 14, 16, 30, 32, 62, 64, 82 and 84, Red Bands.

50c Assortment contains sizes Nos. 12, 14, 16, 32, 62 and 64, Red Bands.

25c Assortment contains sizes Nos. 8, 10, 12, 14, 16 and 30, Red Bands.

10c Assortment contains sizes Nos. 8, 10, 12, 14, 1, 30, 31 and 50, Gray Bands.

COMPO WESTPORT CONN.

THE DEVICE THAT PREVENTS CLOGGING

cOMPo Paper Stapling Machine
"cOMPo—*It will not clog*"

In every office there is a need for a quick working substantial machine that will fasten papers, reports, schedules, bulletins and other documents and do this work without clogging, so as to avoid waste of time, annoyance and dissatisfaction—COMPO is that machine.

IT IS GUARANTEED

The Compo Sales Company guarantees its product to give full satisfaction and stands ready to demonstrate and maintain the genuineness of the slogan "COMPO—it will not clog."

The appointment of The Brown Bros. Limited, as Canadian representatives assures special service to the Canadian trade.

Write for illustrated price list.

ACCURATE RESULTS
Secured by Users of the National
NON-SLIP RULER

The ruler is made from flexible steel accurately graduated, having a Red corrugated rubber base, prevents slipping, which is so essential to the user. The combination of steel and rubber used in our Non-Slip ruler makes our product unusually attractive and above all, it assures

EFFICIENT WORK

National Rulers are modern in every respect. They represent the greatest advancement in ruler manufacture. We make them to English and Metric standards. The edges are true and smooth. The rubber is undercut, which avoids danger of inky fingers and blurred lines in ruling.

Catalogue and Price List Mailed on Request

The Brown Bros. Ltd.
Toronto   -   Ontario

1922

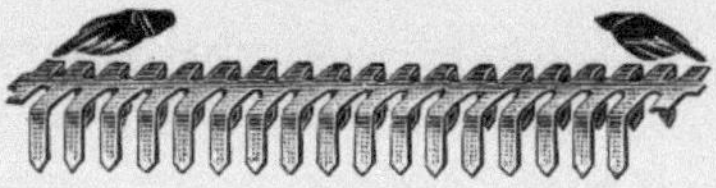

About Hotchkiss Staples

It is sometimes possible to use Hotchkiss Staples in other than Hotchkiss machines. It is *never* possible to use other than Hotchkiss Staples in Hotchkiss machines and secure good results.

Hotchkiss Automatic Paper Fastening and Tacking Machines are designed for use with Hotchkiss Staples *only*. They are made for each other and are guaranteed only when this warning is observed.

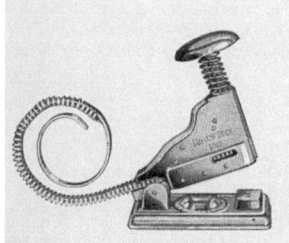

Many other brands of staples are clogging, in f e r i o r imitations—of cheap metal, dull, easily bent, out of alignment, entirely unfit for Hotchkiss machines. At least one staple of each strip is wasted.

Hotchkiss Staples are steel, untarnishable, non-rusting, straight, sharp, strong. Perfectly a l i g n e d with the feeder guide of Hotchkiss Fasteners — *they cannot clog*. Each strip has blank ends so that no staple is wasted.

Genuine Hotchkiss Staples are easily identified by the Blank Ends of each strip, and the Red "H" is on every box. Insist on these!

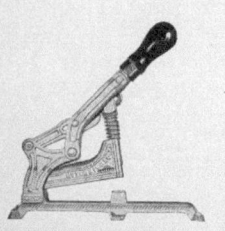

Model No. 1—Binds from 2 to 20 sheets. Most popular machine for every desk.

Model No. 1 Spiral—Same as the No. 1 Model but carries many more staples.

Model No. 2—This machine is lever operated and has a capacity of from 2 to 50 sheets.

Model No. 3—Binds from 2 to 30 sheets.

Model No. 4—Binds from 2 to 40 sheets.

Hotchkiss Tacking Machine—Takes the place of tacks and Hammer. Used in shipping rooms, upholstery shops, window shade factories, warehouses, etc.

1924

Hotchkiss Stapling Machines and Staples

Here is the New Hotchkiss Wire Stapling Machine in two different models.

No. 1A

Fool-Proof and Clog-Proof

No. 2A

USES HOTCHKISS No. 1A WIRE STAPLES
(210 per strip)
Stapling Reach 4¼ inches.
Binds up to 50 sheets of 16 lb. bond paper.
Price, each, $5.00

USES HOTCHKISS No. 2A WIRE STAPLES
(105 per strip)
Stapling Reach 2½ inches.
Binds up to 50 sheets of 16 lb. bond paper.
Price, each, $4.50

These models incorporate the newly devised FOOL-PROOF and CLOG-PROOF feature, that is considered by the best minds of the stapling machine industry to be the most outstanding improvement in its history.

Clogging of wire stapling machines through tampering by inexperienced operators has been completely eliminated by this device. Every effort has been made to clog machines with this fool-proof feature and thousands of staples have been used but these machines have never failed to function perfectly.

Hand Stapler

A NEW and different stapling plier, smartly attractive in beautiful and modernistic color designs. You've never seen anything quite like it, combining as it does, beauty of design with never-failing dependability. So light and handy it rests unnoticed in coat pocket or desk drawer. The magazine has a capacity of 50 staples and 200 staples are packed with each plier.

Price, each, $2.50

Wire Staples

No. 1A Wire Staples come in strips of 210 frozen together by a special process and are packed 5000 in a yellow box. Staples for the 2A Machine are in strips of 105, packed 5000 in a green box. Use these staples only as we do not guarantee our machines unless genuine HOTCHKISS staples are used. Look for the red "H" on the box.

Price, $2.00 a box
Get our price in larger quantities

SPECIAL

We have a few of the old style Model 1A Machines that we are closing out at the special low price of only **$2⁸⁵**

TRIBUNE
PRINTING & SUPPLY COMPANY
Office Equipment and Supplies

Tribune Building　　　　　　　　　　　Phone 4343

1933

Needed in every Store
Star STAPLERS & TACKERS

MODEL 122P
—a handy low price stapler and tacker. Fastens papers anywhere — great for stapling paper bags shut — fits in pocket.
Uses inexpensive standard staples—opens up for tacking signs—shelf paper—window displays, etc.

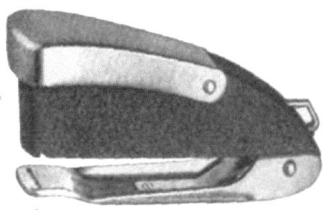

Special introductory offer —
1 Model 122P Stapler and 5,000 staples $2.00
Regular Value $2.75
Money back guarantee

MODEL S12 AUTOMATIC TACKER
No pounding — just squeeze handle—Tacks shipping labels —signs, display material, case lining—dozens of other uses—Twinpoint staple tacks penetrate and hold.

Special introductory offer —
Model S12 Tacker and 5,000 staples $6.00
Regular Value $8.00
Money back guarantee

Star PAPER FASTENER COMPANY
NORWALK, CONN.

1941

Shake Hands
with the TRUE BLUE CLIPPER

Grasp it in one hand. See how smooth and comfortable it feels.

Hold at least two sheets of paper in its jaw.

Press the handles. Clip! In goes a Hotchkiss Coronet wire staple and fastens those papers with an ALL-TIME CLINCH.

Operates as easily as a pair of scissors.

Holds 70 staples to the strip. Stapling range 1".

Backed by the Hotchkiss Unconditional Guarantee because the Hotchkiss Patented Coronet Staples are used.

HOTCHKISS SALES CO. Norwalk, Conn.

circa 1947

1948

1952

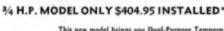

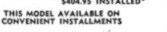

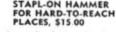

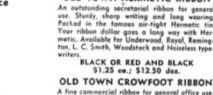

THE E.H. *Hotchkiss* COMPANY
NORWALK, CONNECTICUT
"Pioneers in all that's best in stapling"

Made in United States
Troutdale, OR
12/14/2023